The Sugar Creek Communities

SUGAR CREEK CAMPGROUND

SUGAR CREEK ESTATES

SUGAR CREEK RESORT

SUGAR CREEK VILLAS

SUGAR CREEK COUNTRY CLUB

By John Eacott

This work was created and compiled by John McBride Eacott with assistance.

Copyright 2022 by John Eacott, all rights reserved

ISBN   978-0-9878227-9-6

Orders for copies of this work may be made at www.lulu.com

permission to use extracts may be made from John Eacott at eacott@execulink.com

This work is dedicated to all the people who over the years have put in an effort to make the 3 parks known as the Sugar Creek Communities the success that they have become.

The cover photo is of a 1973 painting of Sugar Creek by Elmer Le Lacheur. It hung beside Bobby Whatley's desk for many years. Le Lacheur may have attended a painting camp run by the campground when it was still very much a wilderness.

V1.0

This book tells the history and the stories of the three Sugar Creek RV parks from the beginning until 2022.

Here in one place is all that has been learned about the Sugar Creek Communities by the author and his helpers.

The production of this history of the Sugar Creek Communities was done with the help of a number of people. My wife Donna and Gary Felts did the editing and proof reading. Gary Felts also did research for the Resort. Dick Anderson contributed for the Villas and Ken Fink did research and compiling for the Country Club. For the Estates, Diane Willis produced some of their historical records.

The photos came from collections in the various parks with John and Barb Lidster providing additional for the Resort and some are from my own collection. Some photos came from the Manatee County Historical Collection. If any material is used contrary to copyright, that use is unintentional or used under educational extract intent.

The author and his wife became an owner in Sugar Creek Resort in 2004 and have participated actively in that park. Those people who have assisted have also been very active in their respective parks.

The reader will naturally be interested in their own park but soon will discover that the other parks share many common events that help in the understanding of the total nature of the Sugar Creek Communities which are for many "Our Happy Place".

                                        John Eacott
                                        Lot 114, Sugar Creek Resort

                                                      Published 2022

Sugar Creek Story

Everyone who finds their way for the first time along 26th Ave E must wonder about their new home in the Sugar Creek Communities.

The destination of 3275 or 3300 or 3333 26th Ave East is eagerly awaited.

What happens when I arrive? What will I do? Will I make friends? Was it a good choice? This is the story of the three parks known as the Sugar Creek Communities and the people who came and called Sugar Creek "our happy place".

We, Donna and John Eacott, arrived in Sugar Creek Resort in 2004 when we chose the park out of many dozens we had considered. We had come to Manatee county to visit friends on Anna Maria Island and we spent several winter trips there before deciding to find a permanent place of our own. So much of our last winter on the beach we spent looking for a park that appealed to us. We found Sugar Creek. The neighbors were surprised because most newcomers came to the park knowing someone. We knew no one. That did not last very long. At almost the same time Marge and Don Crilley had bought just down the street.

When we found the park and decided we liked it, there was nothing for sale so we put up a notice on the board and in a few days we had a call from Rosemary Hutchins. Her friends were thinking of selling and would we be interested in a property beside the golf course? We were!

Soon Bud Rusher and other board members interviewed us and Bud offered to take care of the property transfers with the county. It was common practice for Bud to do this at no charge. There were no security checks, title searches or deposits at that time. If the board members agreed you were OK, you were in. Bud did the paperwork.

There are three Sugar Creek communities in Manatee County. Sugar Creek Estates, Sugar Creek Resort and Sugar Creek Country Club. All are distinct and separate but all have in common the same developer, one Bobby Whatley.

These are the stories about the Sugar Creek Communities.

Technically these properties are part of Section 32, township 34 south, range 18 east in Manatee County, Florida. Currently they are designated in zoning as PD-RV which are parks for recreational vehicles. The Sugar Creek area has had an interesting history. Part of it is told here. It was first known as part of the land of the settler Joseph Braden and then was known as Fair Oaks and still later it was part of the plan of Elwood Park.

~~~~~ *The Sugar Creek Communities* ~~~~~

~~~ *Changing from licence to real property 2004* ~~~

The First People

Our story begins before the arrival of Joseph Braden and any other European people. Long ago, before the Spanish arrived along the Florida coast, the Calusa Indians had established a strong and flourishing culture. Hidden mounds of shells are located on islands and along the coast from this area southwards. These mounds still resemble small hills. There are two at Emerson Point and one on Sarasota Bay across the road from Coquina Beach at Leffis Key which you can visit. These ceremonial high points were the sites of halls, temples and palaces. The Calusa farmed pumpkins, squash, peppers, corn, tomatoes and harvested oysters, clams and fish. Fish were herded with nets into canals and lagoons where they were trapped and kept until needed. A spear man simply walked to the lagoon plunged his spear into the water and picked out his supper. These were tall healthy people who on meeting the Spanish considered them small inferior beings who were up to no good and they drove them away. Unfortunately the visitors brought small pox, measles and other unheard of diseases that decimated the population. Soon there were but a handful of survivors. The Spanish returned. De Soto National Memorial north off 75th street represents a possible landing site for the Spanish invader who traveled deep into the USA.

Seminoles from Georgia seeking to escape their enemies the Cherokee and Creek moved into central Florida and the surviving Calusa escaped to Cuba. Spain passed on this land to England and then it became part of the United States in 1821.

In the 1820's the Seminoles made a treaty to have possession of central Florida. The land was considered low, swampy and useless to the new owners, the United States. Yet by the 1840's the United States decided it wanted the land and attempted to take it away. In the meantime escaped slaves, fugitives, aboriginals and others had created a community called Angola at the junction of the Braden and Manatee rivers. Several hundred people lived here outside the reach of any authority. The United States in 1821 sent in the military to clear them out. Some relocated to the Bahamas, some went back into slavery and some moved on. Actions like this one provoked the Seminoles to rise up and attack the white settlers to try and drive them off their land.

Consequently there were several wars which culminated in the United States passing the Armed Occupation Act of 1842. This act allowed men 21 years of age or older to receive 160 acres of land if they built a stockade, resided there for five years and agreed to join a local militia to defend the land from the Indian claimants. The final major Indian assaults on the settlers ended about 1845 by which time they were overwhelmed by the shear number of settlers. The aboriginal lands were taken away.

The Manatee River was a barrier to travelers going south but otherwise the river was extensively used by boats to travel along the coasts. The Braden River also was a barrier. While it was only 26 miles long, it ran north into the Manatee and created a barrier to travel inland from the Gulf. Thus for most of the time until the late 1880's there were very few roads or people and development mostly took place along the rivers as crossing creeks and swamp land was not so easy.

The first church to be built south of Tampa, representing a growing population, was built in 1887 in the Village of Manatee. It was moved a short distance in 1975 to the Manatee Village Historical park not far from Sugar Creek.

At this time Manatee was not a pleasant place to live. Disease, bugs, oppressive humidity and lack of transportation meant that it was isolated and demanded a high level of self sufficiency in the days before electricity and especially the invention of air conditioning.

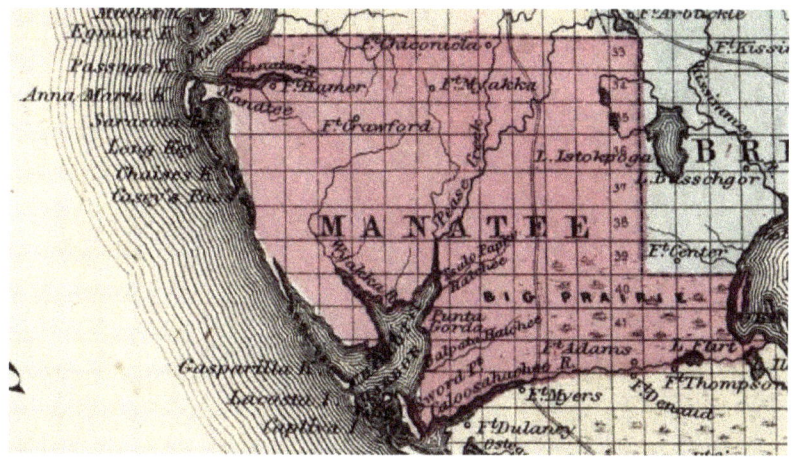

~~~~~Manatee County 1863~~~~~

Behind Local Names

Local streets and locations took their names from the early settlers who tried their hands at various means of making a living. You will know these names because of the road signs. The Johnson family, early settlers, had a son **Morgan Johnson** who held huge tracts of cattle land east of the Braden River. In the 1940's Mario **Caruso,** a New York business man, also bought up cattle land as he had made his fortune as co-founder of the Lionel Electric Train Company established in 1904. He had 5000 acres of land east of the Braden river extending to I -75. Here he raised Brahmin cattle, planted pine trees and grew flowers and vegetables. John Schroeder, a timber merchant, bought up a lot of cheap land over some years in the early 1900's and assembled a huge tract of 48 square miles so he would have lots of land to harvest timber. In 1922 the Uihlein family who owned Schlitz brewery bought this huge parcel and renamed their cattle, turpentine and lumber land Schroeder-Manatee Ranch. The Sarasota Bradenton airport wanted to buy the ranch so it could relocate but this idea prompted a proposal to develop the land as a huge new planned community to be called **Lakewood Ranch** in the 1990's. The airport went nowhere. Lakewood Ranch became a show piece development.

The Reasoner family made a fortune in the tropical nursery business. In 1906 they discovered the first pink grapefruit tree which was part of their Royal Palms Nursery along US 301 at 51st Ave. The AMC movie complex and Sam's Club are on the old Reasoner land along SR 70. The historic Reasoner home was torn down about 2015 as no one would save and move it. A RaceTrac gas station was built on the site. An historic sign marks the location.

A rich woman named Bertha **Honore** Palmer came from Chicago and set up a large ranch in Sarasota, Palmer Ranch. She has a book about her. Honore Avenue is named after her and her name is prominent in Sarasota. Her family created Myakka State Park. A pioneer Cooper family lived on **Cooper Creek** which is now mostly buried under ground around the University Town Center.

A subdivision called Elwood Park was begun in 1916 and recreated in 1924. These small plots were designed for truck farming. They were promoted to be easy "pay as you go" plots for growing celery and other truck crops. One was supposed to be able to make a living with little more equipment than a mule, a plow and a hoe. Today after leaving Sugar Creek on 26th and going south on 45th you travel through the Elwood Park area and its remaining small acreage plots. **Elwood Park Road** is now 38th St. Sugar Creek was considered the northern part of the Elwood project.

In the 1920's the county began a system of naming roads alphabetically. Road "C" now State Road 70 ran from Oneco to the Braden River. A one lane road bridge was built over the river and remained there until 1953.

If a car was coming, one driver had to wait for the other to cross the river. Think about that the next time you drive across the Braden River bridge.

Manatee Road River Bridge early 1940's (now SR64)

The Manatee Road **SR 64** bridge over the Braden river overlooks islands and mangrove which are now conservation lands but in 1999 there were plans to develop all of this area. Only a couple of places were built next to the highway before the council refused to allow further development. So when you cross the Braden River on Manatee and look south you look into natural growth covered islands.

In 1916 the Seaboard Air Line railroad, later Seaboard Coastline, ran a line from Plant City with stops at Parrish, Terra Ceia, Manatee Village, Oneco, Tallevast, Sarasota, Fruitville, Bee Ridge and south with spur lines to Bradenton and Ellenton. The railroad went through land with farms which primarily grew citrus and celery. It was abandoned by the 1960's and the land from the Red Barn to the Sarasota County line was turned into a new US 301 limited access highway which opened in June of 1983.

Samoset was organized as a city in 1926 but many residents of the small town objected to its creation and it was disbanded in 1928. It ran from 26th Ave to Cortez Rd and east to 27th Street. It was thought to have been named after an Indian who aided the Plymouth colony in 1620.

Nearby **Oneco** owed its existence to the Reasoner family. A post office has been in operation at Oneco since 1889. The origin of the name Oneco is unclear but two possible stories exist. One story suggests it has Indian origins and is based on Oneka, the eldest son of Uncas, a Mohegan Indian chief. The second story suggests the Reasoner Nursery was the only company in town, thus **one co**mpany. The Reasoners founded the earliest continuously operated and one of the most important plant nurseries in Florida, dating back to 1881, as the Royal Palm Nursery. The Reasoner's found the original pink grapefruit tree in their farm property near where the Royal Palm Cinema now stands.

~~~ *Reasoner home before 2015 demolition* ~~~

SCR people pass the **Louise R. Johnson K-8 School of International Studies** school on 26th ave frequently. Many Manatee schools are named after outstanding former teachers. Johnson taught in the schools for 42 years and was elected to the school board. She was fond of poetry. She especially liked to quote Frost's poem " The woods are lovely dark and deep...". In 2009 with the closure of Wakefield school where some SCR residents had done volunteer work, the school became the only 100% choice school in Manatee county, 44% Latino 17% black.

~~~ *Louise R. Johnson with a student* ~~~

Sugar Creek and the Bradens

Dr. Joseph Addison Braden arrived from Tallahassee, Florida. He had emigrated from Virginia with his family and 80 slaves. He and his brother Hector planned to establish a sugar cane plantation similar to that established by the Gamble family who lived at Ellenton north of the river. The Bradens had lost their lands in north Florida in a panic in 1837 and in 1842 they decided to go south after learning about the Armed Occupation Act benefits described earlier. The Bradens thus became the first to officially take up land in what is now Manatee county.

The brothers built a log cabin in 1843 near Old Main Street in Bradenton. At first they planted tobacco but their intention was to grow sugar cane. They bought additional land along the Braden river in 1848. Essentially they owned all the land from the Manatee river along 27th Street to 26th Ave and to the Braden River. In 1846 Hector Braden drowned. Rumor has it that he attempted to cross the Manatee River during a hurricane that blew most of the water out of the river. It is thought that he started his ride during the eye of the storm but his horse became stuck in the river mud and then the water returned. According to legend, Hector was found the next day still seated upon his dead horse and he was tightly gripping the reins with his eyes wide open.

Joseph Braden took over his brother's land and continued with the project. He began to build a mansion house and a mile farther south a sugar mill and houses for the slaves were built. It was one of the biggest plantations in the country. They had huge vats where they kept tons and tons of molasses. They constructed many buildings to house their own families and those of the slaves. However for his own home, in 1850, he contracted with Ezekiel Glazier, a cabinetmaker, to build a plantation house and a sugar mill from his own designs. Mr. Glazier's helper was a Rev. Edmond Lee, a Presbyterian minister, who had come to Manatee for his health.

It was reported that while they were working on the house, a Mr. Henry Clark, storekeeper in Manatee Village, died suddenly. Mr. Glazier and Rev. Lee stopped work and went to the Village to construct a casket for Henry. The date on the tombstone, which can be found in the old Manatee Burial Grounds, is July 22, 1850.

The mill was built at a place where the sugar and molasses containers could be poled on barges down Sugarhouse Creek to the Braden River and then to the Manatee where at high tide the containers could be loaded onto boats for shipping. Sugarhouse Creek is what separates Sugar Creek Resort from Sugar Creek Country Club.

Manatee County was created out of Hillsborough county in 1855. This new county included all of what is now Sarasota, Hardee, Charlotte, Desoto and parts of other counties which now exist. The boundary ran from the gulf to the Kissimmee River then followed it to lake Okeechobee then turned west to the gulf at Fort Myers. The census for Manatee in 1860 listed 600 white settlers and 250 slaves in all of that area. This land was still pretty much very empty.

The still angry Seminoles under chief Arpiola decided to take another poke at the intruding settlers in 1856. The family of Dr. Braden consisted of a girl and two boys, one of whom was named Robert. There was always a concern for their safety in this still wild area. These fears were genuine. On Feb. 25, 1856 a party of seven Indians came to Braden's Castle. A maid happened to spot an intruder and screamed. Dr. Braden and his little son gathered the household to safety where they barricaded themselves in until the danger was over. The Castle was fired on and Dr. Braden returned the fire with Major Gamble's new repeating rifle, wounding one Indian in his arm. The Indians retreated deeper into the plantation a mile away (think Sugar Creek) where the workers lived. They plundered the cabins, stole 14 slaves, some of the slave children, three mules and all of the loot that the mules could carry away. In their flight they dropped a shawl which helped to locate them and lead to their capture by the settler's militia. The local militia returned the slaves.

Mill Creek (now Sugarhouse Creek) was named by Braden who utilized the water for the operation of a stone mill which manufactured the sugar on his large plantation. This is a description of how the mill worked.

"The mill was an ingenious device that operated by gravity. The process consisted of three cast iron rollers mounted on top of a brick tower, 25 feet high. A walking beam type of steam engine produced the power to run the rollers. A boiler, 30 feet in length and 40 inches in diameter with one flue, furnished the steam for the engine. Slave workers carried cane up a 25-foot chute and hand-fed the hopper. The cane was crushed by the rollers the juice ran by gravity into setting tanks and was treated with lime."

The sugar rollers from Braden's mill were taken many years ago to the grounds of the Gamble plantation where they can still be seen today.

Sugar Creek Resort and Sugar Creek Country Club share Sugarhouse Creek. This short stream was navigable to Glen Creek (once known as Braden River Run) so the Sugar Creek communities are likely where the mill and slave quarters were located. Sugarhouse Creek was named by Braden as was Glen(n) Creek. Glen Creek had a two foot waterfall, likely where the culvert is at the Sugar Creek Resort entrance. The Glen was the small valley created in the embankment that featured a clear little stream cut into the rock. It was considered a pretty location and the waterfall area became a popular place to come for picnics. That may be the start of camping at Sugar Creek.

Today in the evening while you walk, you can think of the days when the slaves rested by their evening fires outside their cabins after a day of cane cutting and molasses making right here on the land you walk on.

Hard times fell upon the country about 1857. Daniel and Elizabeth Ladd had heavily financed the Bradens, even lending them some slaves that were used on the plantation. Things were not going well for Dr. Braden. His brother Hector, who had been practicing law, was dead. The Cuban market for molasses was lost and the American sugar market collapsed. Acres of sugar cane were destroyed by corn borers so once again Dr. Braden faced financial ruin as he had debts of $8,412 owing in notes. He was forced to give up legal ownership of the property when the Ladd family foreclosed. They took possession of the land and his mansion house in 1857. However the Braden family were able to remain as tenants until 1864 and operated the sugar mill as best they could hoping to pay off some of their debt.

As the Civil War was under way, the union forces arrived by gun boat in 1864 and destroyed the sugar mill and freed the slaves. The Braden mansion survived until 1905.

The Bradens had had enough and they moved back to Tallahassee and then onward to Texas where Joseph died sometime before 1888. He was never to return to the town to which his name was given.

Two of his children had died but his son Robert and Robert's mother returned to Jacksonville, Florida. During his life Robert came to Bradenton area several times and visited the Castle grounds where he had grown up.

Dr. Joseph Addison Braden's sugar mill in Bradenton, Florida. It was destroyed by Union soldiers and abandoned in 1864. (1901 photo) This is the kiln tower of the mill which was still surviving on the property of Col. Charles H. Foster east of Mixon's orchard.

The local community had not forgotten their original settlers and later a group decided to name a new village after the family. The post office misread the name request and for some time it was called Braidentown. That was later changed to Bradentown and about 1924, after someone suggested a better name would be Bradenton, the current name was adopted.

Braden Castle, the ruins of the mansion, also has a camping related history. After the first World War automobile tourism appeared. The early car campers and trailer enthusiasts were called Tin Can Tourists. In 1919, the Tin Can Tourists club was founded in a park in Tampa. This was in the time before motels. They got called the "tin can tourists" because they ate out of tin cans while camping, or they drove Model T "Tin Lizzies". No one really knows the real story. The club was composed of mostly middle-class empty nesters with some time on their hands. During the winter they began camping in Florida. A group who camped near Tampa found their way to the site of Dr. Braden's mansion ruins and in 1924 bought his property and divided it up into 200 40x40 ft. lots. This was the beginning of the mobile home park industry in Manatee county.

In 1866 the Braden land was sold by the Ladd family to Mrs. Mary Elisabeth Pelot, wife of a local Doctor, for $2000 and it was abandoned. However about 1870 Mrs. Pelot sold the southern half of the farm (some accounts say part went from the Ladd family) to Colonel Cooper who resold to Col. Foster. The hammock land on the wooded western banks of the Braden River was renamed as "Fair Oaks". Foster built an elegant two story mansion and proceeded to plant around 3000 young orange and grapefruit trees on 50 acres of his land. He also had 4 acres of sugar cane. This grove was one of the largest in Florida at that time. Unfortunately the white fly in the oranges, the poor health of his wife, and the cost of his home resulted in the farm not being able to produce enough revenue to keep the farm going. Foster died in 1905 and his land was platted into lots later in 1905.

In 1881 in a book "Notes from Sunland" the author describes Fair Oaks as a mile and a half south of Braden Castle and then describes the location.

" *The most direct route to Fair Oaks is by way of Manatee and the scenery en route is unsurpassed in the land of myrtle and ivy. Leaving Rocky Ford you pass Glen Falls, whose pellucid waters sparkle and dance over rock and through a chasm on their course to the Manatee. Graceful palms with evergreen foliage; stately live oaks draped with pendant moss swaying to and fro in the breeze; girded oaks, gayly festooned from base to apex with ivy, yellow jessamine and Virginia creeper, gladden the eye on either side of the road and orange blossom perfumes the air...*"

So next time you enter Sugar Creek consider the sparkling pellucid water of Glen creek and the pendant moss on those big trees. Too bad the waterfall is gone. I presume the author is referencing the Manatee and Braden Rivers and taking a boat towards Glen creek. It was the middle years of the 1880's before the various sections of Manatee Avenue ran from the Braden river to Palma Sola. Wares Creek and other streams were not yet crossed by roads.

In 1881 the Orange Ridge Baptist church began services and the Reasoner nursery was begun. A sawmill was built along the Braden River in 1888. An advertising blurb about that time describes the "Braiden Creek" as winding like a silver thread amid innumerable evergreen islands that present a view as from a poet's dream.

In 1911 the voters approved the construction of 15th Street. In 1913 the Seaboard Air line railway crossed the river south of 64 to get lumber. In 1914, 53 acres was set up to become a subdivision called the Hermitage in an area of heavily wooded live oak hammock. The owner of the Hermitage dabbled in oyster farming and would send insect specimens to the Smithsonian. In 1916 there was an effort to promote small citrus farms. In 1928 the Boston Red Sox played at the new McKechnie Field and there were plans for a Fenway subdivision along the Braden River that never happened.

Robert Beall opened the Dollar Limit store in 1920 which he renamed the "V Dollar Limit" a name that held until it became Beall's in 1946 the same year that Tropicana was founded to make orange juice. De Soto Square Mall, now defunct, opened in 1972.

All these places were part of the Fair Oak property. One portion of the property was used for mining crushed limestone. On this land in 1927 a large vein of travertine marble was discovered. Travertine is similar to limestone but much harder and valued for its beauty as a building material for counter tops, building facades and flooring. A rail line was built to the property and large blocks of stone were cut and shipped in the late 1920's. The Sarasota post office was built with travertine from this mine. However the depression killed the business and in 1937 the mine was sold and finally ceased operations in 1941. The abandoned property was bought by the city of Bradenton in 1952 for $30,000 to be used as a garbage dump. It was ordered closed in 1977 by the state as it was environmentally unsound. However in the 1980's the city turned the dump into River Run Links Golf Course, a par 70 course, designed by Ward Northrup. It opened about 1985. The club house was named "Runnells" for the city councillor who promoted the idea of a municipal golf course next door to Sugar Creek. The Pirate City baseball complex opened for spring training in 1971.

The bed of the old railway line built to haul the travertine marble shows up on air photos from the 1950's and is known today in Sugar Creek Resort as Glen Creek Avenue. It crossed from the golf course near Cozy Corner and ended about Blue Jay circle. Lumps of excavated rock are still scattered about SCR.

Another part of Foster's Fair Oaks land, his orange grove, was sold to William "Willie" Mixon in 1935. Mixon and his wife Rosa came to Manatee County in 1917 after he had served in the army in WW1. Mixon and William Vick bought 20 acres of orange trees in a foreclosure sale from the bank for $12,000. It was said this was an original grove from 1849 but in a freeze in 1934 it was badly damaged. Mixon opened a small country roadside stand to sell the fruit. Rosa Mixon would take the kids with her and they went to the hotels such as the Dixie Grande Hotel to sell oranges to the patrons. Their business sold 250 000 gift boxes in 1992 under the Fair Oaks brand and they became the largest gift fruit shipper in the USA. The orchards expanded but more than 200 acres were sold for development in the early 2000's. The part of the property adjacent to Sugar Creek was kept as a tourist commercial enterprise.

The mobile home park concept was developed during WWII by Charles Moore who designed mobile accommodation for the military and came up with designs for trailer parks for tourists that had both mobility and a local sense of place.. Interest in these wheeled suburbs skyrocketed in the 1950's and 1960's when Frank Fogarty began designing places in Florida for the Tin Can Tourists, travelers who drove "Tin Lizzies" or model T cars who had been coming since the 1920's. They created a campground at Desoto Park in Tampa and later came to Braden Castle.

Bradenton and Manatee county were quick to see the benefits of promoting tourism and promoted a local tourist club for wintering campers. In 1929 The Manatee Tourist Club had more than 1500 members including a sizeable group of Canadian Snowbirds.

~~~ *The Camp at Braden Castle 1920's* ~~~

Bradenton became one of the leading communities for the creation of winter home seasonal residences in the country.

Fine winter weather was one reason. The frost line was north of Tampa and south of that line frost was rare. For every hour south or north in winter there was a five degree change in temperature. Farther south could be warmer but bugs could be worse. Plant nursery people would ask if you lived east or west of I-75 because inland from the bay it was also colder and some plants would not do well.

Manatee county also had its share of storms, an ever present danger to seasonal living. Hurricanes and floods affected Sugar Creek in 1921, 1926, 1944, 1985, 1997 and 2018 among other years. Glen Creek and Sugarhouse Creek have regularly flooded.

With the arrival of the automobile, tourist camps became a part of the local scenery. However this was very much a rural area. In 1950 Manatee County, which today has over half a million people, had a population of 34,000. That was about to change because the interstate highway system was being built and I-75 would run from Michigan to South Florida. On September 6, 1954 the Skyway bridge opened allowing traffic to come from St. Petersburg and Tampa into Manatee County. This bridge was struck by a boat and collapsed in May of 1980 so a new bridge was built but the old approach roads were left as fishing piers. The retirees and tourists began to flow in. In 1963 I drove over the Skyway and the Manatee river past the new Manatee Memorial Hospital. The road turned left and I followed the old 301, now 15th st., past the airport on my way to visit in Nokomis. I came back this way to Tampa airport which then was a cream colored one storey building where I had to walk out to the aircraft and climb the stair ramp into the plane.

My journey to Florida in 1963 was partly on the new I-75 which we had to leave at Jellico, Tennessee and drive through a depressed area of Tennessee where a sofa and refrigerator were on the front porch of unpainted cabins and where wash tubs sat in the front yard. In one tub sat an old man with a scrub brush as it was Saturday. North of Atlanta I again had to reroute on state highways. When I got to the Florida border, I had to enter the state border inspection station where our car was inspected for illegal citrus fruit which I could not bring across the state line. Now it is a Florida Welcome Center with free citrus juice.

Later the route for I-75 from Tampa was at first planned to cross the Manatee river and go along Morgan Johnson. However the road was actually routed farther to the east where it opened in the fall of 1980.

Until 1975 SR 70 east of the Braden river was still unpaved and the bridge over the Braden river was a one lane plank covered wooden bridge. However the opening of I -75 across the Manatee in 1981 increased the popularity of this area greatly. Until 1970 Bradenton was a small city surrounded by farms and people drove across the Skyway bridge from St. Petersburg to pick oranges and strawberries and go for country drives.

Anticipating the growth the new highway would bring, investors built mobile home parks all around the western part of the county during the 1970's. There were at least 109 parks. There were so many parks and campgrounds that more people lived in them than in regular homes. This created great concern and the county stopped allowing the creation of any more parks by 1979. At the time a 2 bedroom mobile home on a sodded lot could be bought for between $16 000 and $35 000.

The first mobile park was started in 1936 by the Kiwanis club as the Bradenton Trailer Park "the world's largest trailer park". In 1955 this park became the Bradenton Tropical Palms Co-op as a share owned park. It is on 14th St. Lots 40x65ft were sold that year for $900.

One of the first recreational vehicle parks was Horseshoe Cove. The concept of a luxury resort with lots of amenities for those with modern motor homes arriving from the north on the new I-75 extension in the county set the stage for other parks, including Sugar Creek Campground. Sugar Creek Campground had 244 sites for family and group camping when it opened in 1973. Site rentals ranged from $6.50 to $7.00. The campground advertised with a large billboard at the corner of 26th Ave and US 41.Some of the early owners first learned of the campground from that billboard.

Sugar Creek Campground had a history reportedly going back to 1931 but it must have been very primitive because as recently as 1950 there were no facilities and poor access. Local people came to Glen and Sugar house Creeks to gather oysters for eating as there was a good bed of them in those days and kids would wade out and swim to Pine Island.

When people come to see Sugar Creek and stand on the dock or cross the bridge in the Country Club, they find a waterway lined with bushes that have in some places been cut off above the water. These are the mangrove which line the coastal waterways of south Florida. These semi aquatic small trees are a tropical plant and they do not grow much farther north than here. The most common of the three species is the red mangrove which is an important part of the coastal eco-system. This area is the edge of their northern range and they are a protected species. It is illegal to remove them but they may be pruned; however, pruning requires a special permit from the state as pruning must be done a certain way. The red mangrove has hanging roots from the branches and live in the salt water. Black mangrove don't live in the water. White mangrove are small trees without aerial roots and are not known to grow locally.

Mangrove along Sugarhouse Creek.

~~~ *1940 aerial photo of Sugar Creek communities.* ~~~

In 1940 when the preceding photo was taken, 26th Ave E ended at 33rd Ave. A trail led to the SE into a property and another trail went north. The road did not cross Sugarhouse Creek nor did it cross Glen Creek. There was some sort of excavation or earth alteration at the site of the Villas and another in the golf course swale next to Cozy Corner. A possible abandoned rail siding or a road enters the Resort from the golf course side and may afford a crossing of Glen Creek at Blue Jay island. There is no evidence of there being a campground across Glen Creek.

Until 1970 there was very little on the land we know as Sugar Creek. An aerial photo from 1950 indicates a few trails, the remnants of a railway spur line entering SCR from the north along the boundary between the golf course and Pirate City. The trails may have been used for campsites and a road went across Glen Creek by 1950.

1950 air view looking north. Photo shows all 3 sugar creek properties, Mixon's, part of Pirate city and golf course. White lines indicate roads and trails, dark indicate streams. No buildings can be determined. There was no pool. The Estates was very wooded. The orange groves are in rows and 26th ave crosses the creek.

A little later another air photo from 1968 shows the development of the Pirate City ball diamonds, Mixons and the city dump as well as a large treed area with a little bit of Sugar Creek in the far left possibly showing the pool area. 26th Ave is barely visible. So in its earlier days the campground was a heavily wooded area without any facilities. Campers came pretty much self contained. (The Manatee Public Library maintains a digital collection of maps and photos available online. These photos from the library may be examined in detail there).

(1973-4 Sugar Creek Campground office)

In 1972 the property known as Sugar Creek Campground Resort consisted of a vacant 27 acre tract that was popular with seasonal campers. Bobby Whatley and his then partners, Warren B. Pearson and Sidney R. Wilkinson, bought the property June 8th 1972 and spent a lot of money to enhance it. The new Sugar Creek Campground opened in 1973.

A pool was built, a meeting hall was built, two washroom/laundry buildings were added and it featured a mini golf, shuffle courts, a tennis court and other amenities including a store where milk and bread could be bought. There was also a barbershop included in the store. Visitors gained entrance to the park via a toll booth and they could camp for a day or a month. School groups would rent the pool and picnics could be held for the afternoon. The park was advertised in camping magazines and featured as a KOA campground. The Airstream campers held their national convention here at least once. Other events such as a bluegrass festival in 1976 were promoted to attract attention and bring in more attendance.

Sugar Creek Campground   Post Card 1970's

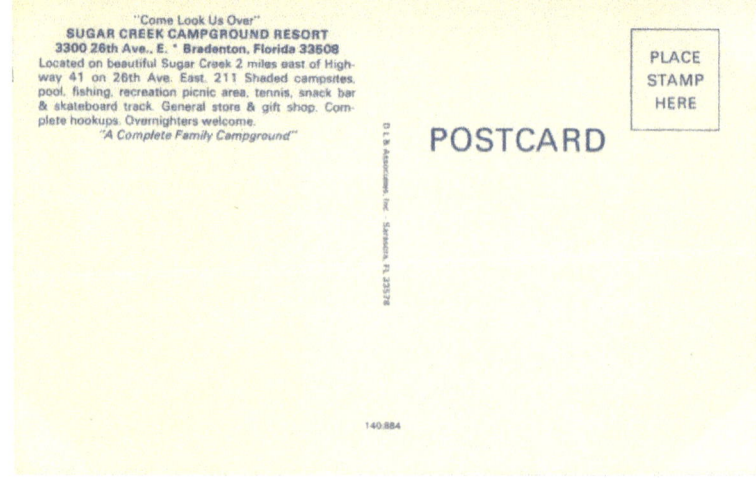

Description:
The back of the card reads, *"Come Look Us Over. Sugar Creek Campground Resort. 3300 26th Ave., E. Bradenton, Florida 33508. Located on beautiful Sugar Creek 2 miles east of Highway 41 on 26th Ave. East. 211 Shaded campsites, pool, fishing, recreation picnic area, tennis, snack bar & skateboard track. General store & gift shop. Complete hookups. Overnighters welcome. A complete family campground."*

Sugar Creek Campground opened in February 1973 as a travel trailer park. The property housed just over 200 hookups on 27 acres located adjacent to Sugarhouse Creek, an offshoot of the Braden River. In 1976, a resident cooperative was founded to operate the park called Sugar Creek Estates Inc. During the 1980s, a portion of the park shifted from being called Sugar Creek Campground to Sugar Creek Campground Estates then to Sugar Creek Estates, the name by which it is known today. Sugar Creek Estates is a 55+ Mobile Home Park and was located in the Elwood park area. (This postcard and comment is courtesy of Manatee County Historical Records Library as are some other included photos.)

~~~ *A Complete Family Campground* ~~~

(The back of this business card was for the Sugar Creek Campground Resort and Estates with address and Bobby N. Whatley, tel (813) 747 6331 or 746 7628)

January 1977

The Estates

The property adjacent to the campground was a riding stable featuring trails through that wooded property. The riding stable went broke and Whatley and his partners, who already owned Sugar Creek Resort Campground, were able to purchase the stable and land about 1976 and turn it into the Sugar Creek Campground Estates. The preliminary plans submitted by William Swan were approved by the county Sept. 1, 1976 for 202 spaces on 17.34 acres. The county accepted this without comment.

The idea was to sell campsites to the campers for permanent use. Owners could bring their trailers and occupy them for 30 days whenever they wanted. The Manatee ordinance only allowed campers to remain for 30 days even if they owned the lot.

There were some initial issues with the Mixon orchards because of crop spraying but that was resolved by establishing a buffer zone along that side of the property. Both the Estates and the Resort were heavily wooded at that time.

Originally the stable farm had a road entrance off of 26th Ave. E. but Whatley relocated the entrance to be next to the Resort and that street address was 3300. This resulted in a common access road to both parks and later the Villas.

Campsites were created and the essentials such as electric service, water and sewers were installed. Picnic tables were provided to each campsite. This was not to be a rustic campsite but a deluxe site on the model of Horseshoe Cove farther down the Braden River near SR 70. A club barn, pool and shuffle courts were created. In 1977 a scheme, which involved his manager Frank Freddes, was conceived to generate more income by selling campsites to the campers. This scheme resulted in the creation of the Sugar Creek Estates Association of owners. Whatley was one of the original board members and remained so until the lots were all sold. An official opening was held and the new campground had post cards printed up for advertising. The first cement pad in the park was poured at lot 77 in 1977.

The original sales list included lots 1-22 along the creek, then lots 56 to

77 around the south and east edge as well as the lots around the club house and to the east. The largest part, all that west of 30th street, had not yet been put up for sale and were still rental lots. Lots 70 to 77 sold for $6,000, 89 to 95 for $6,500, 66-69 116-118 and 133-137 for $7,500, 56 -65 and 139-43 for $8,000, 7-13 sold for $9,500 and other lots sold for prices in between except for lots 14 to 20 which sold from $ 10,000 to $16,000 each. Apparently it was very easy to sell these lots as the entire park was sold out in a couple of years.

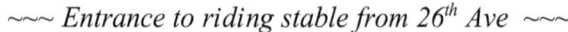
~~~ *Entrance to riding stable from 26th Ave* ~~~

The above photo is looking north and was taken early 1970's when this was a riding stable. Then there is a photo showing what the campground looked like before it was a campground. Then following that is a photo taken from lot 179 of the Estates and shows the same area where the house was looking south after 1974 when The Estates were developed as a campground. The Resort campsites which were developed later looked quite similar.

~~~~ *Sugar Creek Estates before it became a campground* ~~~~

~~~~~~~ *Lot 179 looking south toward 26th st E.* ~~~~~~~~

About 1980 looking east from above Mixon's orchard. Estates club house is shown in center near the right. The Country club is all bush. Golf View drive and Cozy Corner is on the left side. Sugar Creek Resort is partly seen.

The Story of the Estates began with the purchase of the riding stable not long after the campground was purchased. As it was adjacent to the Sugar Creek Campground it was used by the campers for horse back riding as well as for hay rides around the property. When it was muddy the hay ride passengers would have to get off and help push the wagon free.

The one way street system was a product of poor planning as the park was laid out for camping and narrow roads were acceptable when it was a campground. The developers were not professionals and their project was designed to make more money out of campsites. What they created evolved into the three parks over many years. More on the Estates is written later.

Post card from the 1970's showing the club house and solar heated pool

~~~~~~~~~ Campsite 1970's about lot 141 -142 ~~~~~~~~~~

SUGAR CREEK R.V. COUNTRY CLUB is located on the west coast of Florida, bordering the Braden River, in Metropolitan Bradenton. A luxury R.V. park, in the Sun, at affordable prices.

SUGAR CREEK COUNTRY CLUB offers fresh water fishing in the Braden River, salt water fishing in the Gulf for the fishing enthusiast. Sunworshippers can enjoy twelve months of Sun, enhanced by cool breezes from the Gulf in the summer, and southern Florida Sun in the winter.

Baseball fans will delight to having the Pittsburgh Pirates training camp within walking distance from SUGAR CREEK. Many enjoyable hours can be spent watching your favorite major league team play the Pirates.

The best reason for being at SUGAR CREEK COUNTRY CLUB is the recreational facilities offered for your enjoyment: A 6000 sq. ft. clubhouse, with a variety of planned activities, exercise equipment, Sauna Baths, A lovely swimming pool, A therapy pool, tennis courts, horse shoes, pool table, ping-pong, and bumper pool provided to create a country club atmosphere.

We invite you to join us at Sugar Creek Country Club for the rare experience of luxury at afforable prices.

Original Promotion Flyer for SCCC

The Country Club property is assembled.

Before 1980 Whatley and the Sugar Creek Management and Maintenance Company purchased a 50 acre tract of agriculturally zoned land adjacent to the campground which was to the east across Sugarhouse Creek. This was essentially an overgrown pasture with scrub brush. On September 3rd 1980, Whatley and his partners met with the Manatee County Planning Commission and were seeking to have the land designated as T3, a travel trailer park. They wanted to develop 380 campsites on a useable 48 acres. Because the land was low the commission member noted that sewers could be a problem and there was concern about flooding. There was also concern about hazardous chemical spray crossing onto the site from the adjacent farm. Whatley assured the members that the proximity to Mixon's orange grove had not been an issue with his other two projects, Sugar Creek Resort and Estates.

Whatley went on to say, "The proposed Sugar creek Country Club land is abutted by Mr. McClure's pasture and he has no intention of having cattle there for a couple of years."

A further members question about growing tomatoes resulted in this answer from Whatley. " We have been in Sugar Creek Campground for 10 years and Mr. McClure has never grown tomatoes there".

(Mr. McClures pasture land forty years later became the Evergreen housing subdivision.)

The conversation then turned to issues about the campers staying too long to which Whatley said " Sugar Creek has been in discussion about the length of stay. There is a need for varying lengths of stay. Sugar Creek does allow for a six month stay and we may be looking at a park that does violate our existing ordinance because the existing ordinance calls for a 30 day stay maximum. Due to the fact that this is an expansion of Sugar Creek it is going to follow the same patterns. Sugar Creek does not in essence permit 6 month stays. Sugar Creek is a Co-op campground; it is sold, in essence, by proprietary leases. The bylaws of Sugar Creek require the individuals, and it is a manner in which they accept the use of the property, 30 day stays. This is in conformity with the existing ordinance. At the time we originally developed the first application of Sugar Creek this was discussed with Mr. Frank Fisher who was planning director at the time and with Mr. Fay because we knew we could not go in and have a year around lease because the zoning ordinance does not permit it but there is a requirement under the proprietary lease that an individual's stay in Sugar Creek, while he may have a right to use it for a period of a year his continuous stay cannot be for over 30 days. We are considering that there may be a change permitting longer stays and that is why we are showing 20 and 30 foot rights of way instead of the 12 and 10 foot. We are trying to design a facility that would meet the requirements as we know them now that might be imposed for a park having longer than 30 day stays."

So it was in the minds of the owners to alter the use of all of their property so that the owners of the lots could live on them for extended periods of time. Clearly the law said owners could only stay for 30 days. It is now accepted that people may be permanent residents.

Mr. McClure then spoke. " We have not grown tomatoes in a few years but we want to retain our options as to the agricultural use. We intend at some future time to grow tomatoes and use hazardous chemical sprays." The hearing was closed and the information referred to committee.

On Oct 1, 1980 it was again deferred. Tomatoes were never grown there again and in 2018 a housing development was approved on McClure's land.

We return to the Country Club and Villas story later in this book.

SUGAR CREEK CAMPSITE RESORT

Described real estate in Manatee County, Florida, to-wit:

Lots 2,3,4 in the SE 1/4 of the SW 1/4 and Lot 1 in the SW 1/4 of SE 1/4 of Fair Oaks in section 32 Township 34 South, Range 16 East, Plat book1, page171, of public records of Manatee County, FL and the East 50 feet of the SE 1/4 of SW 1/4 of SW 1/4 in Section 32, Township 34 South, Range 18 East, lying South of Glenn Creek, LESS and EXCEPT EXCLUDED AREA. Together with an easement for ingress and egress over and across the excluded area.

*Bradenton
1949*

Sugar Creek Resort Campground

On September 7, 1972 Manatee County received a request for a preliminary plan to create Sugar Creek Resort Campground to be located at 3300 26th Ave E. The county stipulated that the developers maintain a 50 foot setback from all adjacent properties. Sidney Wilkerson represented the developers. The primary reason for the set back was the fact that Mixon's orange groves were next door and they sprayed pesticides on their trees. Spray drift was an issue.

On March 13, 1973, the county gave final approval for the creation of Sugar Creek Travel Trailer Park which became Sugar Creek Resort Campground.

The campground was reported to go back to 1931 but as an organized place to camp it could not have gone back before 1950 as there was no access from 26th Ave before then. Between 1950 and 1972 any camping would have been an activity without any park amenities.

When the campground was purchased in 1972 there had been some trails made and the campsites had no services. The buildings were constructed after 1972. In order to maximize the income for the project, various promotions were undertaken including becoming a franchisee of KOA campgrounds. As Whately did a lot of camping he was familiar with KOA.

It was around 1962 when KOA founder Dave Drum noticed an abundance of station wagons and early-model RVs overnighting on the side of the road or in church and retail parking lots. The Great American Road Trip was thriving but campgrounds were nowhere to be found.

Drum owned some land in his hometown of Billings, Montana. He asked travelers what they were looking for in the way of overnight accommodations and he created a commercial campground on his property, complete with electric hook-ups, central shower facilities, a convenience store and views of the Yellowstone River. Four years later, the first KOA franchise was established in Cody, Wyoming. Success in Cody led to increased franchising efforts. Soon KOAs were popping up all over.

KOAs were exactly what the traveling public was looking for—a clean place to spend the night and the security of knowing that they could leave their belongings to take day trips to nearby parks and attractions. For $1.75 per night, campers could pitch their tent on a campsite that included a picnic table and fire ring. This first campground also provided hot showers, restrooms and a small store. The campground was quickly successful and by the summer of 1963, Drum, Wallace and their partners decided to create a system of campgrounds throughout North America. They named the company Kampgrounds of America and began selling franchises.

By the end of 1969, KOA had 262 campgrounds in operation. By 1972, 10 years after KOA's creation, KOA had 600 franchise campgrounds. By 1980 there were over 900 KOA campgrounds The Arab oil embargoes of 1973 and 1978 caused the collapse of many travel-oriented businesses and campgrounds were in financial need of promotions to rent their sites.

We don't know exactly when Sugar Creek Resort Campground joined KOA but Bobby Whatley and his partners Warren Pearson and Sidney Wilkinson were the officers of Sugar Creek Campground Resort Ltd. It was clear they were following the model of the KOA franchise with their new facilities. Whatley was the driving power behind the campground.

~~~~~ *Southeast Camping Directory 1975* ~~~~~

limit: 50¢. Showers. Recreation room. Reserv deposit required; refund notice 1 wk.
(305) 872-2443
BRADENTON (G-3) 33505
Sugar Creek Campground Resort (√)   Open all year Tent...48...163........RV
1¼ mi s on US 41 & 301, then 2½ mi e on 26th Av E, at 3300 26th Av E. 30 acres. Open,
partially shaded & wooded sites; well off hwy. Fee: $4-$4.50 for 5, extra person $1.25. E-163;
A/C or heater 50¢; W-127; S-127, 50¢. Disposal station. Showers; laundry. Groceries. Htd
pool, fishing, boating, dock, rental boats, playground, recreation room, tennis. (813) 747-6331

In order to promote the park, conventions of RV clubs were held, including some national conventions of the Good Sam and Airstream clubs. The park was getting known.

In 1976 a bluegrass festival was held. At that time the manager of the park was H.L. Brown. He said they had 2 tracts of land available for camping, one with 200 spaces. There was a parking area of 18 acres and there were 33 acres for the festival itself. The festival was a success.

~~~~~~~~~~~Blue Grass Festival 1976 ~~~~~~~~~~

On September 1st 1976 an expansion of Sugar Creek Campground was submitted by William Swan to Manatee County as a preliminary plan for approval of 202 category T3 trailer camping spaces on 17.34 acres. It was approved without comment. These were the first official steps to create the Estates project. No directors of the project were present.

The next year 1977 the Sugar Creek Resort park went through a reorganization and the promotion of activities. The operations manager was Frank Freddes who had come from the west. The planning was to create a park where people could have long term rentals. There were to be two types of park residents, summer and winter. The summer rates were lower and designed to attract locals who would come for a few weeks. There were sites for tents and pull out campers. Originally there were 136 lots. There were no lots in the two circles as these were intended to be used as campfire areas.

The rents were to be $1000 for a year although people could come for the day and rents were 3 dollars per day. It had to be made clear that renting for a year entitled the renter to leave their trailer on the lot but they could only occupy it for 30 days. It also appeared that the county was not of a mind to try and police when the renter was or was not using their camper.

~~~ Art Camping by Tennis Court 1977 ~~~

Frank Freddes, operations manager, thought that a better financial deal could be to sell off lots and make the park a condo association. He had known of this type of arrangement when he was in Colorado. The partners thought that this would be a good idea. So the 5 investors put up $10, 000 each so that the Estates property could be turned into a condo development property. Two parallel schemes were in the works at the same time.

Still the owners were trying to find ways to make the campground profitable and it was being run as a recreational community as the following advertisement from 1977 shows.

On March 13 1977 an advertisement 6 x 6" was placed in the Bradenton Herald which read as follows:

The New Sugar Creek Family Campground
(Now under the management of co-owner, Bobby Whatley)
3300 26th Ave E., Bradenton

Announces
Spring and Easter
Family Camping Fun Special
Reserve 9 nights camping: (12 noon April 7 thru 4 pm April 17)
- **45$ per family** (no size limit) -
Other specials available for fewer nights

Here is what you get:
Free Tennis- Shuffle - Swimming - Basketball - Volleyball - Boating - Mini Golf - Soccer - Bingo - Dinners - Pancake Breakfast - Dancing - Sunrise Services - - Egg Hunt - Contests - - Games and Prizes - **ALL NINE DAYS** For All Age groups

Ask us About group camping, your camping picnic facilities
Call early for reservations 746 7628 , 747 6331

The Campground on paper was a going concern. It had something for everyone. When the mini golf course was created, they hired a specialist who designed and set up the course. Players could come to the park just to play and everyone had to pay a fee to use the course. The caddy shack was the booth for the mini golf. The park was designed to be self sufficient and a convenience store and hairdresser were in the building now used as an office and library. Across the road from the office was a cement pad where there was a propane station and a dump station for trailer waste.

At first the creek was not accessible because of the dense growth of palmetto and mangrove. A clearing was made for both a dock and a boat launch. A pontoon boat departed every Friday morning to take people out on the river for fishing. There were boats for rent. A cement pad with lighted tennis courts was built. Horse shoe pits and four shuffle courts were built. The star attraction was the large lighted pool with diving boards and a life guard. The pool could be rented for special groups and was popular for school groups. There was a cement skateboard track behind the tennis courts. A basketball pad was located between the tennis and shuffle. A pinball game room was between the club house and pool. Playground equipment was located between the pool and the club house. Some facilities were free but others like the mini golf were fee paid.

The facilities were advertised to include other things whose locations were not clear. This included a spa and sauna, a game room and exercise rooms.

Activities were created for the benefit of the campers as well as for people who would come and spend the day. This was not always a welcome situation for the campers because the day visitors had different interests and on weekends the pool and other activity centers could be quite busy.

There was a large BBQ oven and pig roast spits used by campers and groups. Special events days were held such as corned beef and cabbage dinner on March 17th. Square dance lessons, volleyball games and full time craft lessons such as painting were planned for the campers. Group picnicking and club camping were promoted. Each night at 5:30 there would be a bicycle parade for adults and kids to ride around the park.

The club house had a kitchen with short order cooking selling items out a north side serving window. The library at that time was also in the club house by the (then) much smaller kitchen. There was a covered area with picnic tables which is now an enclosed room facing the pool. At some point the hall was extended to the east, the area with a lower ceiling. The central floor area was a wooden dance floor. At one time solar black pipe water heating system for the pool was placed on the roof but it proved inefficient.

Red and Doris Evans were employed to look after the property, the store and the gate among their other jobs. As campers were pretty much isolated the park had a barber/hair dresser, a library, and a store which on one side sold milk, bread, tin goods and on the other side camping gear and tools. The office was also in the same building.

Campers were comprised of locals wanting an outdoor experience and Snowbirds who wanted to escape winter.

.   *(pool, diving board, and play area with club house 1974, notice that the back of the club house is shorter than what exists today.)*

~~ The Neil McClures of Canada camped here in 1977 ~~

During the week the campers had the park much to themselves but on the weekends lots of locals would come for the day as well. In particular school groups in busses would come and party and swim for the day.

There were two campfire circles where large bonfires were built for getting together with others. Large logs were laid out around the circles for seating. There were no camping spots on the inside of the circles.

After dark a night watchman was on duty to patrol the park. The park was not in a very good neighborhood and a fence went around the perimeter next to the city dump and Mixon's orange grove.

Some areas of the park, particularly Cozy Corner, were popular for campers who wanted some privacy back in the bushes. This area was designated for tent campers only.

All park users had to pay to enter the park or show you had paid by displaying a pass. There was an entrance booth about half way up the driveway before the electric gates that allowed entrance into the Estates and the Resort. This was on the left side of the driveway as you came into those parks. An attendant whose name was Red checked everyone at the booth and sent the new camper to the office to pay their fee. One could rent in either the Resort or the Estates.

~~~~~~~ *Camping at Sugar Creek Campground 1975* ~~~~~~~

Rules and Regulations (1970's)

Rules and Regulations for all Sugar Creek Campgrounds.

We ask all to cooperate with these regulations to keep a happy and pleasant park.

- Emergency messages only will be delivered. All others are posted on message board in the store.
- Only one sleeping unit per site
- Check out time is 4 PM Summer. 12 noon Winter
- No rent or sale signs

- No screen tents without permission
- No tents or converted school buses
- Minimum unit length is 18 ft. Maximum length 35

CAMPING
- Our quiet hours begin at 11 PM to 7 AM. Please respect your neighbor. Keep radios and tv's turned down.
- Positively no alcoholic beverages (beer included) will be permitted in the recreation area, store or office.
- Campfires are not allowed
- Clotheslines for swim suits are permitted only at your campsite
- Automatic gate operated by key card only - when closed

SWIMMING POOLS
- Bathing suits only are allowed in the pool
- Swimmers must shower before entering pool
- Feet should be showered when entering pool from grass area
- Those having sun tan oil on will shower before re-entering the pool
- No rafts and no "hard" items (balls, frisbees, etc) allowed in pool
- No food or drink is allowed in pool area
- No alcoholic beverages

PETS
- No pets are allowed in any part of the recreation areas at anytime.
- Pets must be on a leash and cleaned up after
- No pets shall be left unattended
- Pets are to be walked on doggie walks ONLY

ROADWAYS
- Speed limit within the parks is five (5) miles per hour
- Motorcycles, motor scooters etc are for transportation in and out only
- No vehicle should be parked on the roadway or on adjacent site (unless you have paid full rental fee for the site)
- Excess vehicles must be checked at office
- No parking on the grass.

VISITORS
- All visitors must register at office.

~~~~~~~~~~

It is easy to see that some of these rules became part of the new co-op thinking.

One reason the rules and regulations were put in place was the fact that some campers created problems for others and one incident in 1978 resulted in the police being called to evict the occupants of one of the lots. This is a photo of that event.

There was a transition period where there was a mix of co-op owners and renters. Not until the lots were all sold was the ownership transferred to the associations.

The Estates lots were largely sold off by 1979 and the selling of the Resort lots, their primary property, began as a plan to create another condo association. What was not included were all of the common ground facilities which had been included with the more limited common property in the Estates. This was later to create a problem.

At first the promoters thought they would try and sell 50 lots per year. The project developers operated on a limited budget so Whatley would hire cheap labor or do part of the work himself. As a result some interesting residue remains from those days. The streets in the Estates were narrow dirt lanes. The lots were designed to be rented out and so the roads were too narrow to be two way streets. When Whatley opened up the Villas he personally drove the bulldozer to clear the land. In the Resort, Whatley hired a bunch of kids to install the water lines to the lots.

As a result over the years there have been issues with lines coming apart and leaking. In some cases the campers were hired to carry out tasks. In one instance Ed Pederson, a camper was hired to redo the wood floors of the SCR club house.

Lots were sold off for $ 9,000 to $ 13,000. Maintenance fees were set at 15 to 18 dollars a month. In order to sell the lots there was a rent-to - buy program. The campground was not a very good money maker so selling off the lots made sense.

The layout of the Estates being as it was essentially a totally new development was rather straight forward with rows of more or less similar sized lots equipped with parking, a picnic table, and utilities. The Resort was an entirely different situation. As a campground with lots nestled in and among trees the lots had evolved by drawing lines around a camper and spacing it equally from the next one. This resulted in a large difference in lot sizes and so this accounted for the price differential. As the lots were being sold off it was decided that more lots could be created in the two campfire circles. These were the last lots to be created in the Resort and explains why the lot numbering seems unusual.

The lot sales proved to be quite popular and as the sale of Resort lots was winding down the developers attention was placed upon the creation of the Country Club.

In the mean time the Villas property was part plant nursery, owners could leave potted plants there while away and the developers grew plants. The Villas land was for a time the last area where short term campers could come for weekends or short holidays.

Sugar Creek Country Club and Villas

On Nov 13 1980 Manatee County approved 398 travel trailer lots on 44 acres of land to be known as Sugar Creek Country Club. A 40 foot buffer zone along the adjacent agricultural land was imposed and this resulted in a reduction to 378 lots. However on August 18 1981 the buffer zone was eliminated and the 398 lots were restored. At a county meeting on October 1st 1981, representing the developers, Bobby Whatley had said there had been no issues with spray drift from the orange orchard and that the farm, Mr. McClure's land, adjacent was only pasture and he emphasized there were no plans to grow tomatoes or other crops. He wanted to eliminate the spray drift concern.

The length of time people could stay in the park was another issue. The Sugar Creek organization had been in discussion about the length of stay. There was a need for varying lengths of stay. Whatley said Sugar Creek does allow for a 6 month stay and he admitted that they are looking at a park that does violate the existing ordinance because the existing ordinance calls for a 30 day stay maximum. Due to the fact that this was an extension, the same patterns would be followed. He pointed out that Sugar Creek does not in essence permit six month stay because Sugar Creek is a co-op campground; it is sold, in essence, by proprietary leases.

The by-laws of Sugar Creek require the individuals, and it is a manner in which they accept the use of the property, 30 day stays. Whatley went on to say that this was in conformity with the existing ordinance. At the time they developed the first application of Sugar Creek this was discussed with the planning director because it was known there could not be a year around lease because the zoning ordinance did not permit it but there is a requirement under the proprietary lease that an individuals stay in Sugar Creek, while he may have a right to use it over a period of a year, his continuous stay cannot be for over 30 days. Whatley said they were considering that there may be a change permitting longer stays and that is why the plans were showing 20 and 30 ft rights of way instead of the minimals that are existing in the current zoning of 10 and 12 ft. He said, "We are trying to develop a facility that would meet the requirements as we now know them and that might be imposed for a park having longer than 30 day stays." He also informed the county that no screen rooms would be allowed in the travel trailer park or the campgrounds.

Mr. McClure spoke and said they had not grown tomatoes for some years but wanted to retain their options as to the agricultural use to grow tomatoes and use hazardous chemical spray. The planning committee deferred a decision at that meeting but two weeks later the approval came and the Country Club could proceed. Just exactly when it was decided to allow owners to use their lots as they wished is not known but it was clear that ordinance enforcement on individual owners would be difficult.

The above section becomes of interest because the Sugar Creek communities are RV parks and not mobile home parks. This becomes important in a number of ways including the taxes levied and how other ordinances of the county are applied. The fact that they might become permanent residences was clearly not the desire of the county in 1980.

There were 2 or 3 phases to this if the Villas are included. The much smaller Villas was a separate entity at first intended to be only a campground. The Villas did not share the recreation facilities for the Country Club which were located on their side of the creek. A picnic area was the only amenity for the Villas community.

On May 27 1982 the final plan for phase 1, a total of 9 acres, of Sugar Creek Country Club was approved by the county on the condition that utilities first had to be installed. This section was known as the Villas but its completion took place after Whatley sold the project.

On October 22, 1982 Phase 2A and Phase 2B Sugar Creek Country Club were approved as a Recreational Vehicle Park. It began with 237 lots on 26.12 acres.

The five streets closest to 26th Ave were laid out and developed first. This included Maple Drive around the perimeter, Bottlebrush Avenue, Golden Rain Drive, Rosewood Lane, and Tallow Place. Phase two included the remainder of the property. This time the developers had an open field and proper street widths and county standard utilities were installed. A foot bridge to access the clubhouse was built over the creek. Whether this bridge took into consideration that the water was technically navigable to 26th street is not know as its construction would have involved the federal government. The original plan was for the pool to be located in front of the club house but instead two smaller pools were constructed and the size of the parking lot reduced. The Country Club was still designed as an RV park but with the look of a mobile home park since it was anticipated that the 30 day stay would be removed.

Sometime after this Whatley and his company transferred the development to Charles and Don Bencin and others.

~~~ *Original SCCC entrance gate* ~~~

~~ *The Estates horse barn which became the recreation hall* ~~

The Early History of the Estates

In early 1977 the Estates project was underway. Post cards were printed to advertise the park showing pictures of Airstream trailers neatly parked by their picnic tables and their rustic barn clubhouse and pool with solar panels on the roof. They were distributed in the spring and summer of 1977. On the back the card said " a new concept in adult campsite ownership, owned and operated by the campsite owners as a non profit cooperative. Located on 17 wooded acres with luxury campsites and complete recreational facilities." Included was the address: Sugar Creek Campground Estates, 3300 26th Ave E. Bradenton Florida 33508. Buyers were found and the first cement patio pad was poured for Gordon and

Agnes Hooper on lot # 77 in February 1977. The Estates co-operative project would move quickly over the next two years.

In 1989 a committee was formed in the Estates to document their early history. What follows are extracts from that document.

THE FOLLOWING COMMITTEE, AT THE URGING OF HANK MINTZ, SPENT MANY HOURS GATHERING THE INFORMATION FOR THE HISTORY. WE FEEL IT WAS WORTH THE EFFORT.
Dorris King, Chairman
Joyce Lightner
Yvette Monroe
Mim Turner
Introduction by Betty & Mac Macauley, Cover by Pauline Kinzie

A HISTORY OF SUGAR CREEK ESTATES, BRADENTON, FLORIDA

The following is a chronological list of events which have occurred at Sugar Creek Estates since its beginning in 1977.

It started out as an R.V. Park - but with a difference. You could own your own "pad" in a condominium-like agreement (99-year lease of individual lots with common ownership of roads and facilities). When two-thirds of the lots were sold, an association comprised of all owners took over management of the park from the developers.

There were many struggles while learning how to take care of the park and its management, but with the love, cooperation, helpfulness and caring of all concerned owners, the growing pains were lessened and finally the current seven member board of Directors was established as the Governing body of Sugar Creek Estates.

The atmosphere in the park didn't just happen. It has been nurtured by the "old timers" and enhanced by the newcomers as they become active participating residents and the "glad to be here" feeling rubs off on them. The old-timers were RV'ERS - and all true RV'ERS just naturally say "hello" to their neighbors and a willingness to help your neighbor is an accepted practice. So that feeling of love, friendship, companionship and caring was a part of the beginning and is the "stuff" which makes this the great park that it is.

There is a pride of ownership that keeps all lots neat and attractive. There is cooperation between all members which makes the atmosphere that of "It's a pleasure to be here" kind of place. There is a willingness of all to volunteer to help out with their special talents and abilities for the benefit of all concerned. This is a park of congenial people who are willing to accept you as you are and are willing to give of themselves to assist their neighbors. There are always helping hands when anyone is in trouble. There is no substitute for that feeling of support when it is needed and it's always here in this community. The warmth of fellowship is evident the moment you enter the gate and receive a smile, a wave or a greeting. When returning to the park after an absence, the hugs and salutations ..."It's so good to see you"."Welcome back! We've missed you." This is the "glue" that holds us all together and makes us glad to be a part of this place.

When people from all walks of life and from different states and countries can get together and live in harmony, it is proof that traditional values and moral responsibility are still thriving in our society.

~~~ *Lot 77 Gordon and Agnes Hooper pour the first cement patio on February 7 1977 in the new Sugar Creek Estates* ~~~

1977 Beginnings
The first activity of the new owners was to create a social committee.
Coral Methnor - President
Edith Robinson - Vice-President
Helen Willis - Secretary
"Frankie" Wolf

The Social Committee existed before the board had been created.

The Park was incorporated as SUGAR CREEK CAMPGROUND ESTATES ASSOCIATION

Right away the Social Committee began the following activities :
Crafts, Dance, Bingo, Horseshoes, Golf, Pot Luck Supper, Bible Study, Shuffleboard and Cards. Other activities began in the spring of 1978.

In the new year of 1978 the Association was able to put together the first board of Directors.

FIRST BOARD of DIRECTORS: 1978
Jeff Robinson - President
Walt Conover - Treasurer
Agnes Driggers- Secretary
Warren Pearson
Bobby Whatley representing the developers

FIRST SOCIAL COMMITTEE:
Don Jung - President
Joyce Lightner - Vice-President
Inez Davidson - Secretary-Treasurer

The First General Meeting of owners was held in February 1978. The owners paid $9.00 for a mailbox. A ceiling was placed in the barn in order to convert it into a recreation hall and a storage area was organized upstairs. The social committee started the on-going purchase and improvement of clubhouse furniture.

~~~ *The mail lady delivers the first letter January 1978* ~~~

1979 Changes and Events
During 1979 park model trailers were permitted in the park. The maintenance of the Estates was withdrawn from Bobby Whatley and managers were hired. Lot #1 was purchased from Bobby Whatley thus ending the developers role in running the Estates. It was now owned and run completely by the co-op. Office equipment was purchased and an L.D.C. contract was signed for office and maintenance staff. The Social Committee organized an Easter sunrise service and breakfast and the first soup night was held after Thanksgiving.

1980 Changes and Events

The Board ruled that all contractors must present an insurance certificate before working in the park. It was decided that the streets would have one-way traffic in the park and street and speed signs were installed.

A major project was getting the clubhouse painted. A contract to have the solar panels for the pool heating panel replacement was made. The Board started a tree care program under direction of the State Forester. A Christmas Pageant (recited and sign language) "Christmas by Candle Light" was held. Among the firsts that year were a popcorn party, pancake breakfast and Tupperware party. Blood pressure service was provided twice weekly, Sunshine Committee, and Bridge games.

1981 Changes and Events

The developer Bobby Whatley was no longer involved with the operation.

The old solar panel for the pool was replaced for $1,860 in February. A new 24 hr security gate and guardhouse was installed. New clothesline posts were set in concrete. Each unit was assessed 30 dollars for debt retirement and a monthly fee for owners was set at $37.75 per month. Sliding glass doors were installed in the ante room of the club house now called the recreation building. It was decided that all complaints had to be submitted to the office in writing and signed by the complainants. The purchase of big kettles for the kitchen was begun and the recreation committee contributed $400 toward the cost of the pool cover. The highlight of the entertainment was the Womanless Wedding comedy show. By this time the owners of the Estates had pretty much set up their park in a manner that was satisfactory to them.

1982 Changes and Events

During this year a new maintenance contract was awarded to L.D.C. Associates. "Arab" company was awarded the contract for termite-proofing the clubhouse. The owner's maintenance fee was increased to $45/month and a new laundry area was opened. A new roof was put on the pool pump house and new pool covers were placed. Side vents were installed and 2 exhaust fans were put on the club house roof. Among the firsts for 1982 were a flea market, luminaries, name badges and a sing along.

~~~ *New laundry area 1982* ~~~

1983 Changes and Events

The irrigation well was finished and the electric gate completed. A Sharp copier was purchased for the office. Glass doors were installed in the patio area. A sound system was installed in the clubhouse and emergency lights were also installed in the clubhouse. Two P/A speakers were purchased for use in cars for cruising announcements to residents. New activities included organized trips, cribbage, a weekly printed "News &

Views", a CPR course and the recycling of papers and aluminum cans began.

~~~ Well Irrigation System 1983 ~~~

1984 Changes and Events

During this year the cable TV was in operation. There was a $30 assessment per unit for heat & air-conditioning in the clubhouse. New showers were installed in rest rooms and 2 storage buildings built in rear of the clubhouse. Again pool covers were purchased. A Coke machine was placed in laundry area. A fire hydrant was installed. A first aid kit was purchased. An owners' list was made available. It was reported that the park saved $10 000 in water and sewer costs with the new well.

The recreation club activities included the purchase of new pool furniture and a cassette player for the clubhouse. A cook book activity was started. New coffee pots and tables were bought. Bridge tables were purchased. A maintenance fee for copy machine was paid. Bulletin boards were installed in the ante room. A Las Vegas night party was held.
"Hoot" and "Toot" (Great Horned Owl) was born in park.

1985 Changes and Events

1985 was the year that trash pickup by Manatee County was approved. Trailers were now approved with factory installed shingle roofs which were common on park models.

The owner's monthly maintenance fee was increased to $55 per month. Insulation was installed in the clubhouse ceiling. An open and close timer was purchased for the gate. Above ground water valves were installed to access county water and the Estates water lines were disconnected from those of the Resort. A gas stove and hood were approved for the clubhouse and double sinks were installed in the kitchen.

Activities this year included floor exercises and aerobics and a church service was started in the clubhouse. Ice cream socials started as well as a swim suit sale. The cook book project was completed. Coffee mugs were for sale. There was a ham & bean supper and a "Nifty Fifties" celebration. A skin cancer clinic was conducted by a physician. Sugar Creek Sports Fashion show was held and an Easter egg project started for blind children. A lock was installed on the walk-in gate.

1986 Changes and Events

1986 saw some surprising changes. The Estates address was changed to 3275 26th Ave E to allow for more efficient mail service. As well there was an official name change by amendment to Articles of Incorporation to Sugar Creek Estates, Inc.

New paneling was installed inside the clubhouse. The Office and Board Room air conditioners were replaced. The clubhouse was stained. Handicap bars were put in showers & toilets. Seven new street lights were put up in the park. Vent turbines were placed on the roof of clubhouse and handicap parking and ramps installed. A timer was installed in the laundry area. A freezer was purchased. Three new ceiling fans were placed in clubhouse. Center steps were installed at both entrances of clubhouse. Four chair carriers were purchased. A hanging bookcase was installed. A flower planter was installed at gate. Louvered exhaust fans were added in ends of clubhouse. Euchre, pool exercises, line dancing and an Easter egg hunt were begun. A Bingo machine was purchased.

1987 Changes and Events

1987 a fence was constructed around the pool. It is needed when the pool is covered (State Law). Roof was put over shuffleboard seats. Electric service in clubhouse was replaced. All owners were assessed $500 lot assessment for new electric service. Large print Readers Digest were added to library. Bids were taken for individual service contracts.

Thanksgiving & Christmas boxes of canned goods were created for the less fortunate. A Better Hearing Institute program was held. Other firsts were a Hawaiian night party and a bean soup night. The 911 emergency Service was started. Coffee servers were purchased. Volunteers to help students at Wakeland School and a saving Campbell soup labels program for Wakeland School took place.

1988 Changes to the Estates

In 1988 the roof on clubhouse was replaced as were some solar panels. Owners were pleased that $101 per lot was returned because the electric power changes were installed under budget and the new electric service was completed. An Emergency file for lot owners was instituted. A flood light was installed for the flag and a spot light installed on the gate. New mail room for U.S. Postal Service mail delivery was constructed. A new pool cover was donated. Extensive rewiring of street lights took place. A Park Directory for all 3 Sugar Creek Parks was distributed. There was a chicken barbecue by the Samoset Fire Department. The park continued pool and kitchen purchases.

Glen Creek Flood 1988

1989 Changes and Events

New Postal boxes came into use. A new special net fence is in use for pool area per state code. Trash baskets were installed in lift stations A safe was purchased for the director's room. A lawn mowing contract was signed for 1990 with Metro Lawn Service.

There was an increase in monthly maintenance fee of $5.00. New fans and speakers were bought for the patio area. A can crusher was purchased for the shed. A Park Directory display case installed on east side of clubhouse. A volunteer driver's list was organized for neighbor help.

This concludes the history of the first years of the Estates. Next are the records from after 1989 which were annually summarized in detail by Diane Willis and selections from those records are given here.

The first Directory for all of Parks in 1988

1990 - The laundry area was painted and a new floor installed. Vinyl siding was put on the club house. The horse shoe club was started. A birthday week was celebrated. Cement curbing was placed by the club house. The Corps of Engineers cleaned the ditches.

1992 - No smoking signs were posted. The pool deck was coated by volunteers. A gate and concrete pad and two dumpsters were installed. Roads were resurfaced and 11 ½ MPH speed signs were installed. Pool furniture was repaired or replaced.

1993 - The walk through gate was digitized. Ottomans for the pool area and bike racks and refrigerators were donated. Dusk to dawn area lights along common ground were installed along 26th ave. Glass enclosed bulletin boards were installed in the club house.

1994 - A no trespassing sign was put up at entrance gates. It was voted to not allow any type of car port in the park. A Wednesday yard trash pickup in addition to 2 garbage pickup days was begun.

1995 - Both restrooms were completely remodeled. Four new street lights were installed in the two center streets. Eight trees were trimmed or removed. The pool solar system was completely replaced. The old office was converted into a library and all new lighting was installed in the clubhouse. New electric bingo display was purchased and a first aid kit installed in the patio area. A collection of a mile of pennies was begun to equip the kitchen.

1996 - Palm trees were removed from the dumpster area and more concrete added. The kitchen was renovated. New entrance light installed and a new brake unit placed on the gate. Tommy Hughes donated a hand made clock for the kitchen. A new gas grill, card tables, coffee pots and food processor were purchased. An emergency response team was organized.

1997 - Rules and regulations changed to allow 6ft overhang on front and to allow 6 x10 front porches. House numbers were painted on the street in front of each unit. The first Unbirthday event was held. Drapes were removed from the clubhouse.

1998 - A craft show was held in February and the Eye Associates did a screening and a life line screening was also provided. A western BBQ and a nifty fifty dinner were held. The mail boxes were cleaned. New shelves were installed in the library and a bench made for the horse shoe area.

1999 - Another Womanless Wedding was held. An attorney explained

Florida property law and procedures. A new well was drilled for outside watering. The lift pump was replaced. A new A/C was installed on a new platform for the hall. A new speaker system was installed in the hall.

2000 - New flags were hung in the clubhouse for Ohio, Canada, and Massachusetts. A score board was installed at the horse shoe site. A pool clock was purchased. 24 new Mity-Lite tables were bought as replacements. Recycling began in the park. The pool was completely refinished. Street lights were moved to better illuminate shaded areas.

2001 - A Kraut and Brats dinner was held. Street lines and arrows were painted on the roads. A trip was taken to the Kennedy Space Center. The office in the club house was remodeled for a computer work station and a computer was purchased. New vinyl fence was installed on east and west side of hall. A new tile floor was installed in the kitchen.

2002 - During the year significant events were spud night, an unbirthday party, shrimp night and a De Soto Park Picnic. Weekly blood pressure checks were taken. A new display case showing map and owner location was installed. New stop signs and speed signs erected. New shrubbery was planted around the hall. The front entrance garden was improved. A new gate to enter the pool area from the south side was created. The Estates has published a newsletter for some years.

2003 - Terry and Connie Lightner made the decision to join Terry's parents. Terry writes, *"My dad and mom, Vern and Joyce Lightner, moved to SCE and bought lot 80 in February 1977. They were part of a group of 6 couples that were the first to buy in SCE. In the early days of SCE they had a manual security gate that the men would take turns volunteering to man through the night. My dad held a board position for a few years but his time was spent mostly as the park handy man. There was not much he could not fix, a talent that saved SCE a lot of money over the years. My sister Verna Kicsak still owns Lot 80 so it has been in the family from the beginning of SCE. My wife Connie and I would come to SCE for vacations starting in 1979 and enjoyed the people and environment so much that we planned to retire and move here someday. Connie and I came down for a vacation in October 2003 from New York and I never went back North. My Dad was diagnosed with cancer in October so I stayed here when our vacation was over to help my Mom care for my Dad and I was retiring from IBM in December 2003. IBM* *allowed me to work from here until retirement. My wife Connie was hired by the board in 2004 as the Administrative Assistant and Bookkeeper and she retired in 2022. I was elected to the SCE Board in 2005 and retired from the Board in 2022. Like my father before me I became the new SCE handy man after he passed away in 2003."*

2004 - The bylaws were amended to do background checks of all new owners. A new lawn care company was hired. The road at corner of lot 95 was widened. The Estates donated money towards landscaping the center islands of the entrance way. A magazine rack was built for the laundry area.

2005 - A meatloaf dinner was held. A Medicare Advantage seminar was held. A men's breakfast choir was organized. A bus trip was taken to the Dolly Parton Dixie Stampede. The entrance driveway was re-paved.
New bulletin boards were created on east and west side of club house. The toilet seats in the men's room were replaced and the lamp post globes were washed.

2006 - Red Hat Ladies went to high tea at the Ritz-Carleton. A new maintenance shed was built on the north side of the club house and the old shed was converted to a woodwork shop. Cable TV was installed in the hall.
A new gas stove and oven and commercial refrigerator were purchased.

The fire department came and installed new smoke alarms in all units.
An email list was compiled. A new storage room was added to the east side of the hall.

2007 - Joycelyn Martin was the newsletter editor. The Resort proposed having a single mutual gate at 26th Ave for all 3 parks. The proposal was emphatically turned down. Eight residents died during the past year. Sixty-six ladies attended the annual luncheon tea. The table decorations and savories and sweets were outstanding. Sally Sanderback did an outstanding job of chairing this event.

2008 - The front entrance and pool fences were painted and white slats were inserted in the entrance gate. New entrance doors were installed in the club house. New chair racks were purchased. The TV was installed on the wall. $500 each were donated to the Salvation Army and Meals on Wheels.

2009 - 2010 records from March to March. A total of 27 events, many of which were special meals, took place over the year. In addition every week there were a dozen weekly activities such as shuffleboard, blood pressure screening, golf, bingo, horse shoes, water aerobics, game night, church at the SCCC, and Saturday morning coffee. In addition there were 3 day trips by the Red Hat Ladies. New ceiling tile was installed in the club house. A 4x6 lighted sign map of the park was installed at the road fork. Smoke detectors were installed in the club house. New sand was poured at the horse shoe pits.

2010 - A cook book was published by the park.

2011 - More patio chairs were purchased and others were donated. Road damage was fixed and paved. A new water cooler was purchased.

2014 - It was reported that 39 residents had worked as volunteers at the Manatee County Fair contributing a total of 306 hours of labor. This was an event that the Estates did for several years.

2015 - The price of dinners was raised to $7.00 and soup nights were set at $5.00. The cycling club traveled the Legacy Trail. A new bingo machine was purchased and a 65 inch TV was installed. A new sidewalk was constructed to the horseshoe pits.

2016 - New white chairs were bought for the hall. The Eye Associates ran a free eye exam clinic. The club house was painted. The Board decided that no lot could be leased for more than 6 months. The streets needed attention and at a cost of $62, 000 re-paving was undertaken. A special assessment raised the additional money as there was only $20, 000 in the reserves for this.

2017 - John and Peggy Stetzel were president and chair respectively

2018 - Bonnie Bergstresser was president and chief organizer of events

2019 - A trip was organized to Ford and Edison museums at Fort Myers

2020 - Covid 19 had a big impact on events in the park

2021 - Bill Monts and Karen Black were president and chair respectively

2022 - The sidewalk and new fence were installed along 26th Ave E.

Effects of Changes in the Estates on the Other Parks

Because of the effort to document the Estates history years ago, we are able to learn of things which to some degree affected the other two parks as well. The Estates pioneered things which soon happened in the other parks. Once the Estates had been largely sold off, the developers began developing the Resort property into a co-op as well.

~~~~~~~ 33rd Street entrance then and now ~~~~~~~

The Early Days of Sugar Creek Resort

Campers at Sugar Creek Campground wanted to make reservations for their chosen lots for the next season.

The Reservation coupons started with a friendly **"I'm Coming!! Reserve space for me at your Campground.**" Here are the details.

Campers were welcomed with a letter from the Sugar Creek Campground Resort. After filling out the application form with all the appropriate details including name, number in party, the type of unit you have, whether you have pets or not, your arrival date and number of nights and what utility hookups you required, you were asked to choose your park. The choices to tick off were Sugar Creek Resort, Sugar Creek Estates both at 3300 26th Ave E or Sugar Creek Country Club at 3333 26th Ave E. Bradenton 33508.

Likewise in a friendly manner, under the park logo, an acceptance letter would come hand signed by Jeanie McCandlish as was this one to Gerritt Zlystra of Grand Rapids MI on November 10, 1976.

"Thank you for your deposit, enclosed you will find your confirmation slip.

We are looking forward to seeing you in January.

All of us at Sugar Creek are wishing you Happy Holidays and a safe trip to Florida.

Jeanie McCandlish"

It was not long before such letters became history. Lots were being quickly sold. It was not necessary to be 55 or over to purchase your lot and use it. All you had to be was a camper who wanted a lot in a Sugar Creek Park. It was not designated to be an over 55 park until later.

Sugar Creek Campsite Resort Association, Inc. came into official being on June 11, 1979. The charter # 747932 was granted by the State of Florida on July 5th, 1979 and it included the articles of incorporation that laid out the way that the park was going to work. This was two years after the Estates began.

The first meeting of the Resort board of directors was 26th of November 1979. The directors were the 3 developers of the park and they passed the Bylaws of the Association at that meeting. Those same bylaws to this day affect the way in which the park operates. There were no unit owners on that board so what the 3 developers wrote up have stood the test of time as very little has ever changed in the bylaws they wrote.

Once the bylaws were created the owners began contacting campers and the first lots were sold in late 1979.

The decision to create the **Sugar Creek Resort Co-op** resulted in Frank Freddes, the manager, and Bobby Whatley, the key developer, walking around the park and asking the renters present if they would like to purchase the lot they were camping on. Some of the campers had used the same lots for years and jumped at the chance. Others did not and some took their time. There was no formal layout of lots at the beginning. In fact this all took place in stages. Lot numbering began with # 1 and #2 was across from it. As the numbering went first around the perimeter the sequence quickly got out of step. So when lot 81 followed alternately from 1 it ended up next to the office on Pelican while 82 was still following the outside perimeter from number 2. To try and bring order back to the layout lot 83 was created across from 82. This worked until the inside row got to Short Street. The outside row still managed the alternate sequence to 212. The inside sequence got tangled up in the creation of the last lots in the circles as it looped around backtracking thus ending up with the lots on Blue Jay added last to number 245. No one has ever admitted to creating this unusual layout that began as a sober simple idea but got out of whack when they tried to go from 82 to 83 leaving the other side of Pelican street without numbers until later. Somehow I can see the plan falling part after a few beers.

However the first 40 lots along Sugar House Street were something of an experiment to see if there was enough interest in having a permanent camping lot.

Lot sizes as explained had a lot to do with who was parked where and the lot was drawn around that location more or less equal distant from the next lot. That way nobody had to move their trailer.

A prospective buyer was given a sheet of questions and answers. Here is part of the document handed out to curious would be buyers.

~~~~~~~~~~~~~~~~~~~

Sugar Creek Camp Site Resort Association Inc.
Questions and Answers

What is the Sugar Creek Campsite Resort Association, Inc?
It is an "Incorporated Cooperative" campground which owns 243 full hook up campsites, a 3000 square foot recreation hall, a 60 x 25 x 25 ft solar heated swimming pool, a shuffleboard court, tennis courts, mini-golf course, skateboard track, fishing dock, boat ramp and other facilities such as underground electrical, water and sewer lines.

What is a Cooperative Corporation?
Florida Statutes (Chapter 719) have established the cooperative which provides for a co-operative form of property ownership where the members of the co-operative, in the case of a travel trailer park, consist of the purchasers of individual campsites. In addition to ownership of a campsite, the purchaser also owns an undivided interest in all of the 28 acre Cooperative property.

Does the Purchaser of a Cooperative Share Actually Own a Campsite?
YES, the record of ownership of the individual campsite and the undivided interest in the common co-operative property is recorded in the Manatee County Book of Public Records and subsequently forwarded to the purchaser by the county clerk's office. The purchaser of a campsite is free to sell or rent his campsite.

Who Controls The Cooperative Corporation Property?
The purchaser of individual campsites constitute the sole owners of the Co-operative Corporation and exercises cooperative management through an Association of Owners, state chartered as of November 1979. The registered name is "Sugar Creek Resort Association, Inc." By law officers of the Association are elected by and from campsite owners only.

What Is The Price Range of the Campsites?
$5,250.00 and up depending on the size and location. Financing is available for up to 75% of the cost.

When I Purchase What are the Maintenance Fees?
A $30.00 per month assessment by your Association covers all costs to own and use a campsite except for the cost of electricity and telephone used by your campsite. The Association limits the maintenance fee, a maximum of $30.00 per month until Dec. 31, 1980. After which time the campsite owners must approve of any increase.

Exactly What Does The Assessment Cover?
1. Salaries of Manager, Maintenance and Repair, Office and Clerical work.
2. Supplies and Equipment, pool operation, janitorial services.
3. Daily garbage disposal.
4. City Sewer and County water
5. Real Estate taxes

6. Insurance policies on the Cooperative property.

Are there Any Restriction on Use of the Camp Site?
Yes, the Association has certain restrictions set forth in the By-laws....... Some examples were given indicating trailers, motor homes but not mobile homes would be permitted. Units must be between 18 and 35 ft in length. Pets on pet lots only. Children and guests allowed for up to 90 days.
(*not all material is reproduced here*)

How will Electricity be Handled?
Each Campsite has its own meter. At purchase a $75.00 deposit and $25 turn on fee. Minimum charge is $3.20 per month. When not in use turn off will generate a turn on fee of $6.00.

What are the Costs Other Than the Price of the Cooperative Share?
1. Three months assessment in advance. 2. Cost of recording title, including documentary stamps, 3. cost of electric meter and deposits. Respectively $30 x 3, $90, $ 100

Can I Hold A Site While I Decide Whether to Buy or Not?
Yes, You can make a deposit that will hold for 15 days a campsite at price offered and get your money back if you don't buy.

~~~~~~~~~~~~~~~~~~~

Sugar Creek Resort lots sold quickly in late 1979 and early 1980 mainly to the people who had been camping there that winter and spring.

As at August 1, 1980 these were some of the lots still available in Sugar Creek Resort.

90 of the 243 were still for sale. 30 other lots had recently been struck off the list on that published date.

Lot 111 sold for $ 5,250. Lot 114 sold for $9 250 and 115 for 6,250. Lot 222 sold for $ 10 250.

Lot 173 and 175 were for sale at $6,750, Lot 224 was $7, 550 Lots 43 and 217 were for sale at $7, 950 , lot 54 and 141 were $8 250, lot 235 was $8, 750, lot 107, 179 and 219 were $8, 950, lot 99 and 187 were

$9, 250, lot 133 was $ 9, 350, and lot 238 was $ 9, 750, lot 178 was $9, 950, lot 17 was $10, 250.

The first lot sold was either lot 38 to George and Theda Allendar of Venice, Florida or lot 32 Ray and Claire House. Jo Blanding says Ray.

Of the first 130 lots sold, 42 were sold to people who lived in Manatee and Sarasota counties for use as get away locations.

The other 87 were sold to people who had to travel some distance to get to their property. The largest group of 14 was from Michigan, 11 were from Ohio, 9 from Massachusetts and New York and then many other places with 1 to 6 new owners from MO, IA, CT, NJ, IL, IN, VA, MN, RI, TN, MD, WV, WI, NB, PA, KY and Ontario, a total of 24 states and provinces.

The next wave of buyers added a few more locations. At the time of purchase the owner did not have to be 55 years of age as these parks were not yet designated as over 55 parks. A few original owners were still in the park as of the Spring of 2020. These include those who bought before 1982. They are Robert and Charlotte Banks, Katie Bennet, Jo Blanding, Dennis and Gloria Colville, Sue Copeland, Ray House, Don and Karen Parsons, Ed Pederson, Lorraine Sivret, Gordon and Rose Marie Spenser, Dick and Alice Starkey, Danny Wiedenhoft.

Dennis and Gloria Colville of Ottawa, Ontario had come to Florida with their 17 foot Sprite trailer to camp in the summer of 1978. They had planned to camp at Tampa as they had in past years but it was raining and they saw in the KOA book that there was another park in Bradenton so they decided to try it. As they came down US 41 they were greeted by a large billboard at the corner of 41 and 26th Ave E advertising Sugar Creek Campground. They turned left onto 26th Ave E and drove to 3300. At the booth the gate attendant "Red" directed them to the office to register. Red and his wife Doris managed the park and store. Red was a true "Salty" character recognized for missing parts of his ears due to cancer. Colville's were assigned lot 100 and set up their trailer on that site. It was a good spot and they reserved it for 30 days the next year. Sugar Creek was a good place to camp. The next year they learned that lots were to be sold and thought about buying but didn't. When they returned the next year, their lot 100 had been sold to John and Rosemary Hutchins and they were relocated to lot 51. After some discussion, Gloria pointed out that lots were selling quickly and if they wanted to be able to come back, they needed to make up their mind. Next door were the Millers and across the road were Virgil and Mary Salm. Both families had just bought. Dennis and Gloria enjoyed these folks company and so decided to buy. The salesman pointed out that their trailer could not be stationary but they had some park models for sale and they could cut a deal. That sounded like a good idea and they became owners of a nice new trailer. Dennis and Gloria returned every winter until Dennis was 93 in 2020 and they decided to sell.

~~~~~ Gloria Colville, Mary Salm, Dennis Colville ~~~~~

Ed and Marjorie Pederson arrived in 1980 from Massachusetts and quickly bought lot 184 in the Resort. Later they made SCR their permanent home where Ed still lived in 2020. Ed recalled the lot he chose had birch trees. They could walk down to the park store to get bread and milk.

Shirley and Dick Oulette left Michigan in 1979 to go to Sarasota to visit

Dick's parents who were the managers of St. Armands Towers. However when they arrived, they found that they could not leave their trailer in the yard. So they arranged a rental at lot # 11. They had never been to the park and arrived after dark. 26th Ave was dark. The road was muddy and there had been a bad storm so there were branches and trees down. They had to set up in the dark with no power. Their trailer was pretty small for 4 people as it had bunk beds and a tiny table. They liked the park and their friends Peggy and Gerry McDonald and Doris and Bill Clarke also helped them find a better lot and a better trailer and helped them move the next year in 1980 to lot 203. Bill Grange, who lived in the park, helped them set up their new trailer. Dick liked to be busy and he helped do the garbage pick up in the park for a long time. Dick died in 2000. Shirley said they liked the dances and dinners especially the Valentines dance with live music. The park held many pot luck dinners where each person was to bring food for ten. Shirley liked to bake and then give cookies away to others so she became known as the "Cookie Lady". She recalled that in the early days everyone had a name tag.

Robert and Charlotte Banks were on a camping trip and during the winter of 1980 decided to buy lot 101. They were one of the first owners. However they also like camping in other places and finally settled in Arizona. In 2019 some 40 years after spending time in SCR they decided to return from their home in Iowa. So for 40 years they rented their lot out and never ever came to camp there again until 2019.

Dick Starkey's father had come from Michigan in 1960 and invested in a 10 unit cabin park on Hwy. 41 on the corner where Millers Restaurant was located. When Sugar Creek resort began selling lots, Dick and Alice bought lots 55 and 57. These lots were nothing but dense brush and trees. Dick came down with two pickup trucks and chainsaws to clear enough space to park their trailer.

Dick and Alice Starkey 2012

Dick and Jo Blanding chose lot 16 because they wanted access to the water and Jo, who had been raised on Tallevast Road when it was a dirt farm road, liked the idea of having a get away place. Like many others they had been campers at the park. They first came in 1973 during the gas shortage. Their business was near SCR but they lived 16 miles east so they bought a camper and spent the weekdays at the campsite near their business and then went home for the weekends to look after the cows and horses. As campers Jo recalls there was no hall or pool but there was a store and post office located between the current office and pool. The store had shelves in the center and on one side they sold paper products and food and on the other hardware and tools. The store was needed because there was no shopping nearby for the campers. There was a fire burning area and the branches and wood from cutting was stored under a metal roof. The Blandings decided to buy a lot on December 16, 1979. Bobby Whatley handed them a hoe and stake and said *"Go pick out and mark your site and put in a post and report back where you are camping and wanting to buy"*. Today Jo has family near SCR where she now lives full time. Dick died in 2019.

~~~~~ Dick and Jo Blanding ~~~~~

Among the first owners was John and Katie Bennett of New Jersey who bought lots 5 and 6. Katie became a member of the first board and for many years audited the books of the recreation club.

When Don Parsons first came here the pool was under construction. The recreation hall had been built and the new office was both an office and a store where ice cream, bread, milk etc was for sale.

Rents were $20 per week then changed to a monthly rental of $200. You could reserve your site for the next season at the current rate if you did it a year in advance. When Whatley put the rates up to $300 then to $400 per month in 1978, Don decided not to renew. However when he went to the office, Lorraine, the girl who worked there, said Whatley was going to sell lots. Don made an offer which was accepted if it was in cash by the next day. He has owned lot 58 ever since.

Some families have gone from generation to generation in the park. Donald and Maxine Wilson learned of the park from Dick and Alice Starkey who were their friends and neighbors in Michigan. Wilson's bought lot 55 in 1981 next to their friends. At first they used a fifth wheel, then they bought a park model. Their son Kenny and his wife Kathy during those early years would come for Christmas and other holidays with their children Jennifer and Jeremy. The park activities appealed to Maxine and Don. Don would play shuffle board with his friend and partner Carl Hodge. Maxine never wanted to miss bingo. For many years pot luck suppers were a fixture in the park and Maxine would make a salmon loaf from the fish Don caught and canned from his catches in Lake Huron. Eventually, when they were eligible, Kenny and Kathy bought their own retirement lot at Number 94 in 2002 and they became active with the board and recreation club.

Back in the 70's when the park was being created as a family oriented campground the first section developed was down by the creek. The area towards Mixons was just a mix of woods and under brush. When Bobby Whatley made a new campsite, a bull dozer pushed out a space and the power wires, water pipes and sewer were buried together in a single trench.

The skate board track was built behind the tennis courts and was cemented in. The skate board track was removed when the lots were sold and it became an over 55 park.

At one time there was no porch, flower bed or bicycle parking area in front of the kitchen. A request was made to have some cement sidewalk put down so there would be a place for bicycles to park. John Hutchins lot 100, with help from wife Rosemary and their son, did the cement work there. John also put in the cement pad by the library where the mail truck parks.

Ray House, an early camper, may have been the purchaser of the first sold lot which was number # 32. Ray and Claire had owned a motel in the California mountains. They sold it and moved to San Diego before deciding to try living in Florida. They were on a camping trip but kept finding all the campgrounds were just located in open fields. Driving down US 41 they saw a huge billboard 60 x 40 ft with an arrow and instructions to turn at the next intersection to go to Sugar Creek Resort Campground. They found the Resort in a camper travel guidebook for KOA. They drove into the park and turned left and found a site on the river that he really liked. The opposite side of the river was lined with alligators and there was a boat launch just a few places down the street. It was the kind of Florida he had been looking for. There were no fishing regulations and he could roll his aluminum boat which had wheels under it into the water and then flip the wheels up. Later the wheels rusted off. Fishing then in Florida did not require a license. As Ray was looking for work, Bobby Whatley hired him to cut the grass in the park including the mini golf and the skateboard track which was cement and grass and located behind units 31 to 43. He met Dick and Jo Blanding who were also camping on the same street. Dick asked him if he could use a ruler. Ray, who had trained as a cabinet maker, thought this was a silly question but he learned that there were people who could not measure a board with a ruler. He worked for Blanding for some years. Some of the work was in the park. At first add on rooms and car ports were not allowed because as an RV park the trailers had to be readily moveable. This explains why many units still have trailer hitches underneath the units. Ray and Dick built many carports and add on rooms of units in the park. Later Ray worked with Bob Campbell who was a great cement contractor who also lived nearby in the park. They did driveways and other projects in the park for some years. A trademark of Campbell's work is a small elevation of about an inch above the street at the end of the drive so when the street is re-paved the cement will not be below the street level.

Flooding could be a problem along the creek but the county began to require retention ponds and storm drains in new subdivisions so street flooding was considerably reduced. This was not a problem for Ray so when Frank Freddes, the manager, told him they were going to sell lots he bought the first one after Freddes had claimed one for his own use. So Ray and Claire were the first buyers of lot 32.

Early in their life in the park Claire had made each of them Santa suits and they would ride around the park for nearly 40 years in their Santa suits every Christmas.

Ray claimed that he helped Whatley create the first bylaws of the Resort, then a one page document.

Hal (Harold) and Kay Virkler decided to tour the USA in their RV after he retired from senior management with Agway in 1981. They headed west from New York state and made their way around the country eventually arriving in Florida to visit an uncle who lived in Bradenton.

They went to an RV park near the airport and found it too noisy so they set out to find another place to camp. When they entered Sugar Creek Resort in November 1981, they turned right after entering and when they passed by lot 21 Kay turned to Hal and said, " There, that lot, I want that lot." They went to the office and paid for their camping and were informed that if they wanted, they could purchase the lot. After purchasing they decided to get a better trailer and wanted a park model with tip outs. Whatley told them the rules did not allow trailers with tip outs so they bought a single wide. However, when they went home for the summer, they returned to find that the rules had changed and tipouts would now be allowed.

During their second winter in 1982 Harold decided to get active in the development of the park. The Estates had organized a recreation and social group and it was decided to do the same at this development. Hal became the first chair of the Recreation Club but he also was interested in improving the basic structures of the park. There were no paved streets and as these lots were being sold as permanent holdings he thought that they ought to have paved roads and better facilities. The electric system was 50 Amp and designed for casual campers not seasonal park models. People found that you could not plug in a toaster and a coffee pot without blowing a fuse. This was not acceptable and so the entire park was upgraded to 100 amp service. More important yet was the fact that as he was a business person, he saw the need for the park to have reserves set up so that future repairs and upgrades to basic services would be done at lesser up front expense to the owners. The reserve system was designed with life plans for buildings and services and money set aside to replace them in due time.

In 1987 Kay made her last trip to Florida as it was their happy place and she died in February while at Sugar Creek. Kay was an enthusiastic supporter of the pot luck suppers every Wednesday night and for many years it had high standards. (By 2007 the local enthusiasm for pot luck suppers faded out. Some were bringing marvelous dishes to feed 10 and others would bring a can of mashed corn. The last pot luck of that series ended when a lemon pie arrived covered in dozens of ants and a chicken dish of incompletely cooked chicken made several people ill.)

Hal had refused to go on the board until after Kay died as he felt she needed his attention. After her death his name was added to the ballot as a write in and he was elected to the board. During these early years until 1995 he was influential as president and board member as well as recreation club chair and organizer of the golf club players. He died in 1999 and was remembered as a smart, able man of great integrity.

Frank and Linda Dominguez, a young couple who liked to camp, came up from Venice in the 1970's to camp along the creek. However when they decided to buy in the park, they found that they had to be 55 years of age so they had to wait until they were old enough to become owners. They both enjoyed working with the landscaping of the park. Frank, an expert wood carver, made many comical wooden Santas which Linda decorated.

An early enthusiast of the parks was a Canadian, tennis playing, minister from the Dutch Reform church who with his contacts in Western Michigan and Ontario actively encouraged those he knew to consider winters in the sunshine of Sugar Creek Communities. It was through his efforts that a significant number of families chose to come. Frank Freddes recalled that in the early days the Canadians were the shakers and movers in the park who built on the work that Whatley had started. The Michigan people were big into landscaping and gardening.

Frank Freddes came to the park in 1975. He was working in Sarasota and heard that the campground needed a resident manager. His first impressions were not good. The park was junky and overgrown. The dirt roads were full of pot holes and the pool was green with algae. The park was a shambles of bobcats and palmettos and vines among the dense trees. Frank went to the store (now the office) and the guy behind the counter confronted him asking, "What is it you want?" Frank did not like his tone and left the store. Someone entering the store recognized that Frank was there for the job and the guy from the store came out chasing after him. Frank agreed to try the job for 30 days if they would also give him a free camping site.

Frank's primary job was to be the resident's co-ordinator. A job that entailed running games, BBQ's , and promotional activities. They held ghost stories at campfires, Easter egg hunts, hay rides, scavenger hunts, and even sack races for 70 year olds.

During the summer he doubled as the maintenance man and a crew with machetes and an axe helped to clear out camping lots. At first it was decided to create 40 permanent lots along Sugar House Street. These were rented out for the summer for $60.00 for the season. Freddes took lot 1, The Blandings lot 16, Ray house lot 32. Later Freddes moved to lot 13. These renters began to ask about buying their lots.

Freddes recalled that when he lived out west some campgrounds had been turned into co-op and suggested the idea to the owners. Whatley and Freddes decided to go to Tallahassee to investigate about creating a co-op campground. The state authorities wondered why anyone would want to buy a lot in a campground that they could only use for 30 days a year. It was finally arranged for 40 lots to be made available for campers to own while the rest were to be for rent. Warren Pearson, one of the owners, who was known for his financial and legal advice, realized that the park had to be improved or the potential and existing investors would pull out.

The wood from the clearing of lots was saved for winter campfires. At one point while working with the clearing crew Freddes was axing a palm tree and the axe head flew into the creek where it remains to this day.

The campsites were just that, places to camp. There was no water, no sewers and no electricity. These amenities were added in sections over several years but were below the current standards. The sewers were designed for small trailers not large mobile homes. The electricity was created for 50 amp plug in circuits not for park models with full air conditioning. Each campsite had a BBQ pit and a picnic table. Freddes and other workers including a mister fix it man named LeRoy were involved with the installation of the facilities during the summer months.

Weekends were quite busy with local groups coming to use the facilities. There could be up to 1500 come to swim and play on a good weekend. The weekly campers found all this distracting. A night watchman was hired to patrol the park and quiet the camping during the night.

Every afternoon at 4 pm a barrel sprayer went through the park fogging for the "no see um" midges. The park went to a local exterminator and bought their commercial fogging chemicals. During this time campers would make themselves scarce to avoid being fogged. While the summer people were of all ages, the winter crowd tended to be retirees who came and spent their winter at the camp. It was to this group that the sales pitch to buy the lots was made. It was planned from the beginning of the sales that eventually the park would be for seniors over 55. However at the time of the original sale this was not a condition. It was an action taken early in the days when the owners took over the park. It took about three years for all the lots to be sold.

The Country Club was a cow pasture. The Estates was a wooded horse pasture and the horse barn was part of a riding stable that people would come and ride horses around the forest there. After Whatley bought the Estates, hay rides were given around the property which had trails rather than roads. When the tractor drawn wagon had a flat tire, the riders had to help push the wagon out through the sandy mud created by recent rains.

The Sugar Creek Campground was divided into trailer and tenter sections. The area in what is now Cozy Corners was designated for tents only. It attracted a clientele of drug users, prostitutes and gypsies who spent their summers back in there. The summer people were locals and were given deals for parking their trailers for the season so they did not have to take them out when not camping. The summer campers were largely allowed to do as they pleased but in the winter the park had planned activities. The winter campers came with trailers from farther away and wanted things to do.

Freddes recalled that before the streets were paved a tractor they owned dragged an old bed spring along the roads to level and fill the pot holes. The campers who spent the winter would drop off their potted plants at the store where they were tended over the summer. Of course they grew and so the next fall the owners would not recognize their plants. A lot of properties were planted with these saved plants that got too big.

In an interview with Frank Freddes, operations manager, he said that the park had 5 investors who put up $10,000 each. It was Frank's idea to convince the owners to make the park a condo association similar to ones he had known in Colorado. There were two types of residents, summer and winter. The summer rates were lower and attracted locals. The sites were for tents and pull out campers. Originally there were 136 lots. The lots in the two circles were not intended for lots but as campfire areas. The rents were $1,000 for a year and day rents were $ 3,00. Lots were sold off for $ 9,000 to $ 13,000. Maintenance fees were $15 to $18 a month. There was a rent to buy program. The plan was to sell 50 lots per year. The campground was not a very good money maker so selling off the lots made sense.

When they put in the mini golf, a specialist advised and designed the course. It was a pay to play course and the green caddy shack was the booth. The existing office was a store and there was a hairdresser available as well. Propane was sold at a station (cement pad) across the road from the office. This was because once you were in the park, there was no place to go. There was an entrance booth about half way up the driveway. The park had a dock and later a boat ramp was built. At first the park was not accessible from the creek because of the mangrove brush. On Friday morning a pontoon boat went out for fishing with any who wanted to go.

The park had a BBQ oven and also pig roasts. Each lot had a BBQ pit. Many locals would come for special day events. On March 17th cabbage and corned beef would be the feature. Large bonfires were held in the circles with large logs arranged to sit on. After dark a night watchman was on duty all night. A fence was built around the park to keep intruders out. A life guard was hired to be at the pool.

When the club house was built, there had been a separate screened area for eating (now enclosed as the Lawson room) and a serving widow to sell take away food was located on the north side of the hall.

Freddes decided to remain in the park as an owner after the management contract had been terminated. He liked the ambiance and the location and the people. However around 2000 he decided to relocate away from the park. When he returned to the park in 2012 to speak to the people of the park, he commented how lovely it was and that it was no longer a campsite but a park of well kept homes and green spaces with lots of flowers. During the period from 1977 until the middle 1980's there was continuous activity by Whatley and the company in developing and selling their three Sugar Creek Communities almost simultaneously.

All during that time until the last lots in section 2 of the Country Club were sold, the Sugar Creek developers made certain things quite clear up-front in each of the parks.

1. The co-operatives were being created on fee simple interests and not on leasehold interests.

2. There is no recreational facilities lease or club membership associated with these co-operatives.

3. The developer has the right to retain control of the association after a majority of the units have been sold.

4. The sale, lease or transfer of the units is restricted or controlled.

5. The co-operative units may be transferred subject to a lease.

6. There is a contract for the management of the co-operative property with the development company.

All three parks were quick to walk away from the development company and in the case of Sugar Creek Resort there was an additional situation.

Somewhere in the above conditions there was an issue that later came to be a vexation for the new owners and that was to do with certain aspects of the common ground and the ownership of the buildings. While the developers were in control of the property before turning it over to the owners to run, they had an extra way to gain leverage over the new owners that did not create a problem until the owners took control.

There was also an issue with an **excluded area** clearly shown on the map in the prospectus. This strip running from 26th Ave East to a triangle back of lots 51 to 63 included the entrance road, the office building and back to and including the maintenance building. From the prospectus it shows the hall and pool were to be commonly owned. The strip was not owned by the SCR association. The purpose of that strip of land was not specified in the prospectus but it controlled the entrance to the park all the way to 26th street. There was a price to be paid for the new SCR owners association to gain control over that bit of land. It was a considerable price of $600 per unit which ultimately was added to each lot's assessment in order to gain ownership of the excluded land, the office and maintenance buildings and the access to the park. This issue came to a head about the time the developer gave up the right to control the association. The co-op members had to buy the excluded area or

Whatley and company could do whatever they wanted with it. Whatley was not going to be the park manger and the owners needed the facilities. The Co-op members felt they had no choice and agreed to buy the excluded area for about $150,000. As a result Sugar Creek Resort became the owners of the private road from 26th Avenue that allowed access to the Estates, the Villas and the Resort. Consequently in order to retain access the Villas and Estates share the upkeep costs of the entrance road (33rd St. East).

The selling of lots and establishing the co-operative was not an overnight happening. A period of a few years was needed for it to all come together.

What appears to be the first unit owner controlled board meeting was held on March 2nd, 1981 at 2 pm in Bobby Whatley's office. Present were Warren Pearson, Bobby Whatley, Harry Moore, Katherina "Katie" Bennett and two members, Frank Cooper and Ralph Holland, who were not yet full members presumably because their lot sales were not finalized. Harry Moore nominated Bobby Whatley to be chairman. Whatley nominated Moore to be vice chair. Moore nominated Katie Bennett to be Secretary and Bennett nominated Whatley to be treasurer.

All voted in favor.

A motion was made to get signature cards for the bank for all 5 board members.

Frank Cooper raised a question about property taxes for each owner and it was decided that each lot owner would get to declare 1/243 of the total tax bill paid in 1980 in the sum of $7,666.96.

The next meeting was to be on March 31 1981 at 2 pm.

It was few months later when the Sugar Creek Resort Association committee actually became the governing board without a developer representative meaning that all lots had been sold.

When the last lots were sold, the ones in the circles where the campfires had been, the association committee took over the running of the park. That was 1982. The first President was Don Clough. The operating budget for the transition year 1982 was $87,000 of which $24,000 was for the management fee. Wages and benefits were another $20,000. The annual fee was $360.00 per unit.

From the beginning the Recreation Club, which likely existed before the actual Board, had a special role not only as the organizers of events but as owners of the park property that was not attached to the ground. When the Co-op association took over the full ownership of the park, the Recreation club became the owners of these items.

The Recreation Club at the transition had 100 chairs, 12 tables, 8 pool side benches, 10 park benches, 2 swing sets, 1 monkey bar, 1 slide, 2 teeter totters, 1 water cooler, 7 four place booths, 1 upright piano, 1 speakers rostrum, 100 song books, 35 hymnals, 1 8ft x 8ft game shed, 3 shuffle courts, 3 tennis courts and ½ a basketball court, 1 skate board park, 3 soccer balls, two volley ball nets, 2 volley balls, 2 basketballs, 7 skateboards, helmets and pads, an 18 hole miniature golf course, 30 golf clubs, 50 golf balls, 1 ping pong table, and 12 picnic tables. All these items had an estimated value of $10,000.

The Prospectus

Every interested person signing a contract was given a half inch thick 14x9 mimeographed document which contained all the details of ownership and the park.

Here are some of the details provided in this document.
Article I
The park was to be a limited partnership under the laws of Florida.

Article II
The development had been created with 245 units on a total of 28 acres with completed recreational facilities. Ownership of a cooperative campsite unit to be transferred by the issuance of a proprietary lease for each campsite. The Association shall maintain a registry of the transfer of the proprietary lease. The Resort is a planned travel trailer campground and lends itself to short term rentals and leases of the individual units.

Article III
Describes the various recreational facilities. A 2967 sq ft hall with 1190 sq ft of covered deck and 152 sq ft. of covered games room. The hall

could seat 250 people and included offices, restrooms, utility room and kitchen. The solar and gas heated pool was 60 ft x30 ft with an additonal diving area 20x20 ft.with a depth there of 8ft. The deck area was in excess of 2249 sq ft. The pool can accomodate 200 people. There were two bath houses of 990 sq ft each with laundry rooms and showers. There were three shuffle courts, three tennis courts and an 18 hole mini golf, a skateboard track and a half basketball court all of which were lighted.

The facilities are part of the common area and each campsite owner owns an undivided fractional share of the equity without lease or membership requirements.

Article IV
Management of the campground. The developers controlled the management of the park and hired a manager for $24, 000 a year. There was a contract for that attached.

Article V
Sale or transfer of units was restricted and requirements were set forth in the bylaws.

Article VI
Control of the Association described the developers' rights until the rules of the Florida statues were met.

Article VII
A long list of 28 use restrictions was issued regarding the occupancy of the unit. These were expanded and clarified in the bylaws.

Article VIII
explained the services and the providers, water, garbage, electricity, etc.

Article IX
pointed out that each owner had an equal fractional share and also liability over the ownership so that 1/243 of the common expenses fell on each owner. Until Dec 31 1981 that cost was to be not more than 35 dollars per month per unit. (There were 245 lots but only 243 for sale)

Article X
explained the operating budget.

Article XI
explained the existing condition of the buildings and were certified termite free.

Article XII
explained the closing costs and what was required.

Article XIII
provided information about the developer.

The prospectus then dealt with the Articles of Incorporation as required under Florida law.
It included that all funds and titles to all properties required by the Association and their proceeds shall be held in trust for the members.
The Association shall have the power to levy, charge, assess and collect fees from the owners as allowed by the lease. There is no power to declare dividends and no power to inure a benefit to any member or director. There was to be one vote per campsite on any decision.

The articles go on to describe the election of officers, directors and the bylaws and methods of amendment. All these details were created by the developers who signed themselves on the 11th day of June 1979.
Walter H. Wyar of 40 South Pineapple, Sarasota
Bobby N. Whatley of 2619 51st St. West, Bradenton
Warren H. Pearson 4803 22nd Ave West, Bradenton

The By-laws of Sugar Creek Campsite Resort Association Inc. are little altered since they were first printed and created. They were not created by the owners but by the 3 developers themselves.

In the beginning there were certain understandings that over time may have become forgotten. One is that the owners are collectively the landlord and their unit is held as a tenant. The price of a proprietary lease is the sale price of the campsite. The Association maintains a registry of all leases and transfers may be made only on the books of the association and the lease initially issued shall be recorded in the public records of Manatee County. All lease holders are subject to the rules of the By-laws. Since the leases are issued by the Association, the Board has control of the transfer of the lease and of any sublease.

The proposed budget for the first year of the park operation was for $87,480 not including unspecified reserves. The annual fee per unit was set at $360.00 or less than a dollar a day.

The budget was roughly broken down to include:

Wages	$20, 000
Maintenance	$ 6, 000
Supplies for recreational areas	$ 7, 500
Water and Sewer	$ 8, 500
Garbage	$ 3, 000
Real Estate taxes	$ 8, 000
Insurance	$ 4, 000
Insect Control	$ 880
Management Fee	$24, 000

It appeared that Whatley had a long term interest in managing the parks as he maintained ownership of the office and maintenance building until the owners of each park decided to do their own internal management.

~~~~~ The Whatley Family about 1978 ~~~~~

Bobby Neal Whatley

As each park took over their management of the park the developers and Bobby Whatley left the scene. By 1984 the Sugar Creek management company, which had managed and run the park under Whatley, had wound down and Whatley went on to do other things. For the better part of a dozen years he had taken an idea and saw it evolve into the three parks that exist today.

Bobby Neal Whatley was from Columbus, Georgia where he was born November 2, 1933 and moved to Manatee county in 1962 where he and his wife Marilyn raised their three girls. At first he worked as a lab technician on Manatee Avenue before becoming a salesman for Curtain Scientific, a supplier of materials ranging from surgical scissors, scalpels, chemicals, scientific instruments to centrifuges. He traveled from Jacksonville to Miami. The company was sold in the 1970's to Coulter Electronics. Whatever his reasons for leaving and taking on the Sugar

Creek project it fit the interest of a social person who was an avid outdoors man.

The Whatley's had a popup camper and nearby Sugar Creek was a popular spot nearby to camp. The family all liked the out of doors and camped all over. His principal partner and friend Warren Pearson and a silent partner took a notion to purchase the Sugar Creek property in 1972. It was essentially an undeveloped property, perfect for do-it-yourself self contained camping. Whately had a vision to create a better campground and turned it into his career. All the Sugar Creek projects were his hands on activities and job. He loved being in the parks. After his Sugar Creek project was finished he managed Winter Quarters RV park which was on the right when you cross the Manatee River on I-75.

The Sugar Creek projects occupied him during the 1970's and early 80's. In the prospectus of Sugar Creek Resort he stated that he had been involved with the construction, development and operation since 1972 and that as general partner he managed the development and sale of the cooperative campsites. Previously he had developed one other cooperative campsite, being the Estates. The Country Club project turned out to be too expensive for him and he sold out to recover his investment. Later he worked for Manatee County as supervisor of the aquatic weed section of the Manatee storm water drainage department.

Bobby was interested in many things, genealogy, the sons of the American Revolution, Trinity Methodist Church where he was very active and because of his daughters, the Girl Scouts. As a teenager his daughter Nancy worked at the store in the summer and on weekends.

Bobby Whatley died 73, (1933 to 2007) Memorial Park, St. was survived by his daughters Dr. Nancy Asheville NC, Laura and Tanya Owens of families.

March 15, 2007 age and is buried in Petersburg, FL. He wife Marilyn, Whatley (Snider) of H. Scott of Bradenton Tampa FL and their

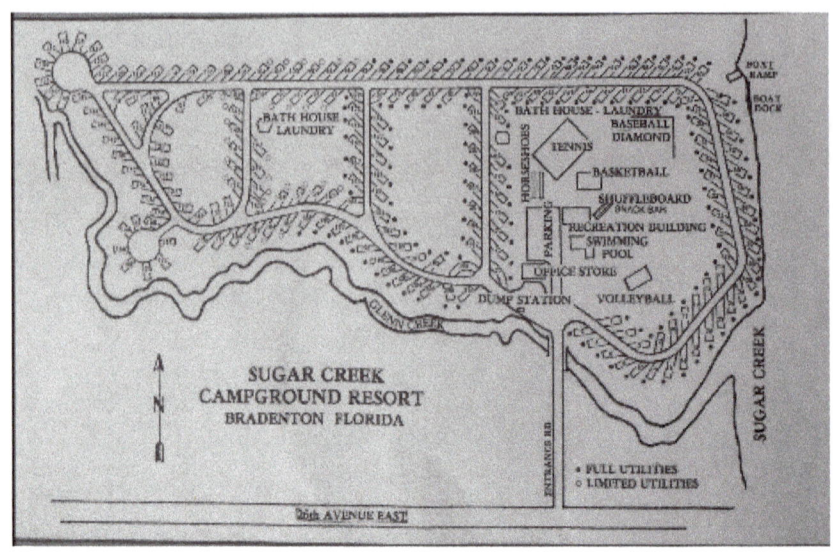

~~~~~~ *1970's park plan* ~~~~~~

~~~~~~ *Pool and Club House 1970's (no addition on back)*~~~~~~

~~~~~ *Shuffle and Horseshoe Courts 2006* ~~~~~

~~~~~~~~~~~~~ *by the office 2004* ~~~~~~~~~~~~~~~~

Sugar Creek Resort Through the Years

March 2, 1981 - The first meeting of Sugar Creek Board of Directors was held. The membership included new owners and the developers, primarily Bobby Whatley. A bank account was set up and positions on the Board were agreed on.

1982 - First president of the Sugar Creek Resort Board of Administrators was Don Clough. It was not a requirement for owners in the selling phase to be over 55 years of age but the park decided quite early on to become an age restricted park. A record for that has not been found as the early years of the park records have been lost. Board minutes exist from 1999.

~~~ *Planting Blue Jay Island before streets were paved. This photo includes Dick and Shrley Ouillet, Bob Butts and Charlie ?* ~~~

1984 - An area of the park which Whatley held as an excluded area gave him control of the entrance road but permission to use the road was given to the Estates and the Resort. In addition Whatley had another deal to allow SCCC to access their facilities across the Villas property. On April 18, 1984 an agreement was made for the excluded property to be conveyed to the Resort. Technically Sugar Creek Campground Resort

Limited conveyed to Sugar Creek Campsite Resort Assn. the land with easements for the Sugar Creek Campground Estates Assn.

This was described as "Lots 2,3,4, in SE 1/4 of SW 1/4 and lot 1 in SW 1/4 of SE 1/4 of Fair Oaks in section 32, Township 34 south range 18 east and the east 50 ft of the SE 1/4 of SW 1/4 in Section 32 lying south of Glen Creek." William DesMarias the SCR president as well as Deborah Greene and Diana Jamieson of Sugar Creek Campsite Resort and Bud O'Brien of the Estates signed the document. So from then forward the Resort was the proper owner of the entrance road known as 33rd Street East but the maintenance was shared with the other parks who had right to use the street.

1985 - Don Clough was the president and it seems that the last lots controlled by Whatley were sold. This may have included lot 77.

1986 - By this time the volunteers of the park were holding regular Thanksgiving, Christmas and St. Patrick's day dinners. Craft sales were also very early activities. 1986 Wood grain tables were bought for the hall.

1987 - The renamed Sugar Creek Association was created on the 18th of February 1987. The Articles of Incorporation of Sugar Creek Resort Association Inc., formerly known as Sugar Creek Campsite Resort Association Inc., were signed on behalf of the members by president Peter H. Large lot 45, V.P. William Grainge lot 204, secretary Harold Virkler lot 21, and Edna Mitchell treasurer lot 39.The officers are to be the Board of Administration consisting of at least 5 persons and must always be an odd number. The first board included the above named plus Don Clough lot 76, Dave Arnold and Roy Wallace lot 233. A total of seven members, a number unchanged thereafter.

1988 - The first 3 park joint directory was published. The new Villas were included in the 1990-91 directory. The directories could be tax deductible. The activities included Horseshoes Monday at 10 am, followed by Crafts at 1 pm and Euchre at 7 pm. On Tuesdays there was Shuffleboard and Exercises at 9 am with Pine Needles at 1 pm and the Club meeting the 2nd Tuesday at 7 pm. Wednesday there was Shuffle at 9 am and a Potluck supper at 6pm and Ladies luncheon noon on 3rd Wed. Thursdays Exercise at 9 am, Bowling at noon and Bingo at 7pm. Friday

Exercise at 9 am, Golf at noon. Saturday 8:30 am Coffee hour, 7pm Ice cream social and 8 pm Cards. Rotational Tennis daily 9 am.
Special activities included dances, craft show, flower funds, and holiday dinners.

1989 - there were wood doors each with 9 glass panes to exit to the Lawson room.

1990 -The Recreation Club became known as the "Sugar Creek Resort Senior Citizens Service and Recreation Club". It was a lengthy title it held for several years.

1991 -John Hardesty who had bought lot 202 in 1988, moved full time to the park in 1992. He had been treasurer of the Board in 1990 and in discussion with Mary Salm he decided to use his experience as post master to arrange for the US Post Office to deliver mail directly to the residents mail boxes. The cost of the boxes which were installed in January 1991 was $4,889. Mail delivery began a few months later. The other parks do not have this level of service. In 1993 John joined the recreation club as treasurer, a position he had for about the next 20 years. John's specialties were helping with aluminum recycling and the chicken BBQ.

~~~~ *The SCR Astro Notes Valentine Dinner Dance* ~~~~
~~ *Don Johnson trumpeter on the left* ~~

1992 - The Board of Administrators on Feb 12 received a letter from the "Sugar Creek Resort Health and Recreation Club" asking for repairs to the mini golf greens. It was decided to add exhaust fans to the bath houses. The dock had to be closed for repairs. It was decided the term for new Board members would henceforth be three years. A pool table was purchased for the library. New units were approved for installation at lot 24 Hughes and lot 46 Campbell. Bob Campbell served on the board and he was skilled in cement work and donated many hours finishing off many cement projects in the park. The Board considered but tabled a plan to have a yard arm added to the flag pole to include a Canadian and a Florida flag.

1993 -

1994 -

1995 - The first farewell chicken dinner was held organized by Rick Vanettten and Gerry Gransma. These continued for about 20 years. John Lidster, Wayne Parker and John Hardesty were active in the Recreation club and participated in many construction projects in the following years.

The Activity Calendar for 1995-96 included welcome back party on Nov 11, Thanksgiving and Christmas dinners, pancake breakfast, shuffle dinner dance, tennis group Valentine's dinner dance, an auction sale, craft show, St. Patrick's dinner dance, golf picnic and farewell party March 30. To many this calendar of activities will seem familiar as many of these activities have continued for many years. While the dinners continue, the dances faded away by about 2015 as did the auction sale.

Among the other activities in 1995-6 were rotational tennis, water exercise, pine needles, bible study, cards, shuffle, crafts, horseshoes, pot lucks, bowling, bingo, ice cream socials, line dancing, jazzercise, golf at Heather Hills and mini golf, coffee and donuts, and church.

The Recreation club leaders that year were John Lidster, Bob Schmidt, Janice Keil and Barb Lier.

1996 - A steak BBQ was organized in February and line dancing classes were started and for some years were run by Art Podgorski. The back of the hall was brown board and batten.

Farewell BBQ from early 2000's

1997 - A woodworking shop was added to the garage and was built by the residents including Bud Rusher, John Lidster, Wayne Parker and others. The new woodworking shop was equipped with various power tools including bandsaw, table saw and lathe. It soon was very popular with owners. John Lidster supervised its use for many years.

Glen Creek flooded so much that water ran over the road. New cement was poured at the garbage area.

The cement tennis courts were painted red and green in December by the tennis players and reduced from three courts to two. They had been painted blue and green. The cement courts had been built without any rebars and thus over the years cracked and shifted.

~~~~~ *Constructing the woodworking shop. At work Bud Rusher, Don Parsons, Wayne Parker* ~~~~~

1998 - the old kitchen was torn out. The new one opened in April. Also that year the ladies luncheon and dress show was held. A new fence was built around the compactor. The hall interior was renovated. There was a pay phone and pop machine beside the water fountain. Pot luck suppers were being held as were ice cream socials. Before the old smaller kitchen was removed there was a serving window on the north wall about where the serving counter is now. When the park was a rental, meals and snacks were served out of this window to campers for a fee. When it became a co-op, it was still used for some events but was closed when the kitchen was remodeled. The small library was off a hall to the south of the old kitchen where there are now storage closets. The pool table once in the hall was relocated across to the office building. New bylaws were adopted April 8, 1998 and notarized by Sharon Frederick the office employee whose husband was maintenance man for the park.

~~~~~ *The Club House 1998* ~~~~~

~~~~~ *New Kitchen 1998* ~~~~~

~~~~~ *Old Kitchen Before 1998 with Doris and Bill Clarke* ~~~~~

1999 - A new library was built in the office building as it had been by the old kitchen in the hall. Later John Lidster enlarged the shelf area.

~~~~~ *The Gates as they were in 2000* ~~~~~

2000 - What is called the Lawson room was changed from a screened porch to a vinyl plastic enclosed room. Originally it was named the Sinnett room after the president who screened it in. The first coffee hour was held by the recycle group. The coffee hour was a free thank you for contributing aluminum and other saleable metals. Over the years a lot of money was earned through their can crushing and dismantling scrap. Shooter and Jake Friesema were among the loyal workers there.

The board was told by the residents that they wanted to end the commercial sale of food from the kitchen. The kitchen had a sales window on the north side of the hall. There is still a cement pad there that buyers would use to stand on to get their order. Also in this year the board decided to reduce the number of official lots to 243 from 245. Those extra two lots are the bath house lots.

The board undertook to repair the entrance gates which were frequently jammed. Dick Lawson added the rocking chair figures later.

2001- The recycle group, Rick Vanetten, Charlie White, Jerry Gransma, Andy Devries, John Lammers, "Shooter" and Jake Friesma built an aluminum recycling shed.

The first 50th Wedding Anniversary party was held with 33 couples, it included all those from 1946 forward who had been married 50 years. This became an annual event at which couples told how they met and showed wedding photos, cake and ice cream and drinks were served and the hall was decorated for the event. Some years the bride was given a rose.

The flag pole island was created in memory of the first president of the Association. It was lighted at night. Over the years it has been modified several times particularly in the year when someone drove a pickup truck right over it before crashing behind it.

A big storm created a huge clean up mess. This was a recurring summer event after hurricanes passed by or there were big thunderstorms.

~~~ *A new cement pad was created by the compactor .*~~~

~~~~~ *Work at the Aluminum recycle shed* ~~~~~~

2002- The fountain was installed at Pelican Island. Entry flower hanging posts were installed. An archway arbor was installed in memory of Nancy Castleman near the office. Commercial groups were brought in for entertainment. Blue Jay Island was bricked around. A new cement pad was built for the compactor. The rocking chair silhouettes were installed by the entrance gates. These were made by Dick Lawson who also created the wooden street signs. Dick was park president in the early 2000's. A bougainvillea tree was planted by the hall. The board had to create a special assessment to repair a crack in the pool, remove the diving board and make other changes demanded by the insurance company. Every unit had to contribute to cover the $40 000 cost. The Recreation club offered a course in making baskets out of pine needles by Helen Buenger. Art Podgorski organized line dancing. Bill Clarke looked after the pool table and Art Vadeboncoeur looked after Bocce ball.

2003 - Art Podgorski lead the line dancing in the hall. Some people took a class with Helen Buenger learning to make crafts out of pine needles. Tai Chi classes were held at the Country Club.

2004 - Recreation chair was Patrick "Rick" Molloy, Board president was Dick Lawson. Pine Tree Island at the end of Short Street had two large trees and one was hit with lightning and had to be taken down. A palm tree is planted there now.

~~~~~~~ Pine Tree Island about 2004 ~~~~~~~

2005 - Recreation chair was Dave Patchkowski. Dave had been organizing the shuffle tournaments and continued to do so for many years. The Board decided to fully enclose and finish the old screen porch and it became the Lawson room. The hall roof was covered in a sealed substance rather than have the shingles replaced. Kris Tuttle, daughter of Mary Salm, begins working as office secretary for SCR.

2006 -The president of the Board was Paul Bennink. The new chair of the Recreation club was John Eacott, Dave Patchkowski vice chair, Judy Brockmiller Secretary and John Hardesty Treasurer. John Eacott introduced the idea of having a newsletter for the park and began collecting emails of the residents. There was some initial concern that the emails could be used for other purposes and everyone was assured that the emails would be kept confidential and not distributed. By 2007 there were more than 60 families on the list. John Hardesty, treasurer of the club, arranged for presentations about forming a neighborhood watch program. A park resident upset with the rules took the park to court and a settlement was reached at a financial cost to the park. New metal chairs were bought for the hall to replace most of the old, also metal ones. Some thought padded chairs would soil too easily. A Valentine's party steak dinner seated 200 people after which there was live music for dancing. Live music was expensive and in time very few people actually danced and they were dropped.

~~~~~ *Shuffleboard Courts 2006* ~~~~~~~~~

2007 - We were informed that we would have to have a digital box or a new TVset as television was going to change in 2008 from analog signal to digital. 80 new metal chairs were purchased. A talent night was held in February. Donna Lawson, the Friendship person for the recreation club for some years, was actively sending sympathy cards and notes to residents. She reported the following recent mailings.

Lot	229	Bob Walters was in the hospital
	228	Bill Searfoss has passed away
	16	Vera Jo Blanding- fell and broke her leg now in rehab
	42	Barbara McCaughey's son has passed away

184 Marjorie Pederson has been ill
188 Shirley Collard has undergone eye surgery
15 Margaret Stalter has passed away
161 Sherrie Payton's husband has passed away

A Recreation brain storm session carried out in March by John Eacott, Kathy Wilson, John Hardesty, Dave Patchkowski created a number of projects that took several years to complete.

A whole new white plastic gate operating system was installed by the board. Much of the work was done by the residents. The entrance was widened to accomodate the new gates. A joint 3 park gate near 26th Ave had been proposed but was turned down.

The Sugar Creek Resort Newsletter was begun by John Eacott and ended in 2021.

~~~~ *Preparing for the new gates 2007* ~~~~
~~ *Fred Evans, Marlin Swartzentruber and Ron Soards*~~

The new gates

Repainting the shuffle courts

2008 - A metal, outdoor clock with 2 faces was installed in the flower bed in front of the office. This was a large face decorative clock which included a thermometer as well. It was visible all around the entrance area of the park. However it had many maintenance issues.

~~~~~ *John Lidster remodeling the washrooms* ~~~~~

New benches were placed in the mini golf and money was set aside for renovations of the mini golf. When the mini golf was created in the 1970's, the park developers hired a professional designer to create the park. The mini golf was a play and pay operation before the park became a co-op. Payment was made at the green shed. Over the years the maintenance of the course has been done by volunteers. Tuesday afternoon was the traditional play time but it is open all of the time. The golf course is one of the reminders that Sugar Creek Resort was once a popular campground. Some organized pastimes have faded in popularity including Bocce ball, horseshoes, the pinball game room, and skateboard park. Gone also is the propane depot, and trailer waste dump and boat launch.

~~~~ *"Accordion"Mike Binder serenaded at the pool* ~~~~

At his own expense Bill Vesters had a professional map of the park created and installed near the entrance. The ice cream socials made $486 and the chicken BBQ $693 and the pancake breakfasts $288. Jack and Rauline Morris have bought lot 62. They are among 14 new owners this year including Sterns, Lanctot, Anderson, Hagaman, Buckhannon.

2009 -After an injury to Jake, the maintenance man, his hours were reduced and the park contracted to have a grass cutting company mow the grass. Jake Zoutendyk was the maintenance employee from the early 2000's until about 2019. A router was donated to the office by John Eacott so library users could have access to the internet.

2010 -Storage space has always been an issue so in January a new Robbins shed was purchased and set up behind the hall on a cement pad created by Bob Campbell. Large capacity laundry machines were installed. Several oak trees were planted to replace some removed including one in front of the office. Every year large piles of telephone directories were dumped off at mail boxes and most had to be taken to the garbage. Outside the park the county opened the school bus depot across from the Estates and a dead body was dumped across the road from the Country Club. It was decided to no longer erect memorials about the park and instead a memorial area with memorial bricks for a patio would be created. Frank and Linda Dominguez did most of the creation work. Frank and John Eacott installed the water sprinkler systems around the park.

~~~ Celebrating the new gates ~~~

2011 - The boat launch was closed due to insurance and maintenance issues. Over the years a number of previously existing facilities had been ended over insurance liability issues. Earth boxes with petunias were placed by the hall entrance and a cement patio was created between the pool fence and hall for use when the pool was closed. The underground water sprinkler system was expanded.

Walter Meixner played his pipes for dinners, birthdays and special events

A big screen TV replaced the 32 inch one in the hall. After much controversy the board decided to build a cover over the shuffle courts but only at the south end. Some objected to the expense, others saw no need.

A year later it was agreed without controversy to also cover the north end of the shuffle courts. The popular cruises to different areas organized for many years in January by a park resident, Rick Molloy became the subject of a complaint by one of the participants that went away when it was pointed out that this event was not run by the park but its organization was allowed as a courtesy gesture because residents wanted it.

The Board members for 2011-12 were Ken Wilson, President; Bill Vesters, VP; Rick Molloy, Treasurer; Carol McLeod, Secretary. Member Jim Meyer resigned and was replaced by Ron Fletcher.

The Recreation Club officers were John Eacott, chair; Dianna Brabson V.C.; Kathy Wilson, Secretary; John Hardesty, Treasurer. John Hardesty resigned after many years service and was replaced with Herb Zuercher.

~~~~~~~~ *South end shuffle cover* ~~~~~~~~

2012 - The Board installed video cameras to monitor some areas of the park. The Garden club begun in 2005 continued with tours to interesting locations around the county. Palm trees were planted between the pool and parking lot. Dick Lawson park president in the early 2000's passed away. The Board installed a permanent dumpster for large furniture items and replaced the garbage compactor. A table tennis was bought for the club house. It was discovered that there was some space behind the hall storage closet next to the kitchen and this was opened to increase the size of the closet to store card tables. Owners were allowed to have golf carts. Security checks were required of all new owners. The area between the pool fence and hall was cemented to make a patio. A highlight of the years was a celebration of the park's 30th Anniversary in March.

~~~~~ *Charlene and Frank Freddes and Kathy Wilson* ~~~~~~~~

The Holly Hills mini golf was renamed to Oak Leaf Run a name proposed by Linda Hannan. A lot of renovation took place on the course. It was decided that renters would henceforth require a background security check. The hall bathrooms were made wheel chair accessible.

2012 Anniversary Event
"Our park anniversary ice cream event held this past March was a huge success. Perhaps it was the ice cream and cake which was provided. We had an attendance of over 160. Our guest speaker kept everyone's attention for over an hour. Frank Freddes, who was operations manager for the old Sugar Creek Campground and one of the originators of the concept of making the park a co-op owners park, had lots to say about the early days of the park. There was also a display of artifacts and material related to the old days including Sugar Creek mugs, a Sugar Creek recipe book and Sugar Creek maps. Photos were taken and will be placed in an album commemorating the event. It will be placed in the library. A video was also made so anyone who missed the talk can view it and learn about the days during which we became an owner run park."

- Extract from the "Sugar Creek Resort News"

2013 - Once again the new sign out by the road has for the 3rd time since it was put up been run into and damaged. The old ones never got hit for 30 years and were in the same place.

The pop machine owner has decided there was not enough money made off the machine so it has been removed. There will no longer be a pop machine by the entrance to the hall. You probably thought the park owned it. They never even gave us money to cover the electricity they used. New shuffle court sign boards were installed. The park held the first Talent Night Feb. 28. A Souper Night replaced the pot luck suppers that had died out after many years. The large fast growing Ear tree by the entrance was removed as its pods were messy and the branches brittle. The hanging basket posts were given vinyl covers. Agnes and Shooter Friesema retired after organizing the Thanksgiving dinner for 15 years. Frank and Linda Dominguez installed a new trailer. It was the first in the park for some years. Renovations began on Blue Jay Island with the planting of a palm tree. Publix opened a new store at 45th and SR 70. Decorative paintings were done to bath house floors by "Char" Krass.

"Shooter" and Agnes Friesema 2012

Gerry, "Shooter", spent many hours crushing cans and aluminum scrap. Agnes spent many hours organizing dinners.

~~~ Painted floor in laundry area by "Char" lot 129 ~~~

The park celebrated several birthdays in 2013. Don Johnson 89 played trumpet in the Astro Notes band. Gord Miller 90 was an avid tennis player and Leroy Taylor turned 99.

2014 - The old cement tennis courts were removed and a new paved surface with tennis and pickle ball markings was installed by Lawson Courts for $50,160. When the cement was removed, it was found there had been no rebars put in to stabilize it. "Char" Krass painted a mural in the ladies shower room. Mary Salm reported on the Friendship cards. Rick Molloy who had served 11 years on the Recreation Club and board gave up producing the monthly calendar. The waste water lift pump was refurbished. New owners will not be able to rent out their units for two years. It was decided to change the auction sale into a garage sale. A well water system was installed to Short Street park. A summer directory was created by Herb Zuercher. A mystery party night was held for the first time. A terrible accident at the Country Club parking lot took several lives.

~~ *Street Party in Cozy Corner for Leroy Taylor's 100th* ~~

~~~~From the left *Marg and Don Crilley, Don and Carol McLeod, Betty Wilkinson, Nancy Berens, Carrie Wilson, Millie Wykstra, John Butler. Below: Francine Lanctot, Mary Salm, Leroy Taylor*~~~~~~~

2015 - The Victorian tea became a popular event. A Facebook page was launched to give SCR folks an open forum for sharing information. The center of the hall floor made of wood had to be replaced with cement and new tile and the painting of the interior of the hall was begun. New stop signs were placed in the park. No one was able to organize the chicken BBQ this year. It was decided to try pickle ball on Wednesday morning if there was enough interest. New playground equipment was bought to replace the old. The new housing project across the road from Mixon's was under construction.

2016 - Park fees were $286 per quarter. More security cameras installed. Committee was formed to look into chair replacement for hall. Nine new parking spaces were created across from the hall. The office complex had a new roof installed. The interior of the hall was totally redecorated in light green, taupe and brown. The entrance to the hall was made wider and the front porch widened by two feet and a new fence was installed by John Eacott and Eric Weiler. A Christmas cookie exchange was created. The doghouse in the mini gold has been rebuilt. After 10 years with the Recreation club Dave Patchkowski retired. Rauline Morris was elected as vice chair. Rinus Dekerk, Ken Wilson and Nancy Berens were elected for a 3 year term to the board. Renovations included a new roof on the office and library area and the installation of new fans and ceiling lights in the hall.

~~~ 2016 new fence in front of hall ~~~

~~~~~~ Pickle ball was introduced in 2015 ~~~~~~~

2017 - New white plastic chairs and storage carts replaced the old metal ones and new white card tables replaced the old ones, A new refrigerator and freezer replaced old ones in the kitchen. Thursday Bingo night was discontinued after 30 years because of lack of interest. Mexican train dominoes were started on Monday nights. A defibrillator was bought for the hall. Rauline Morris replaced John Eacott as chair of the recreation club after he had served for 11 years. The exterior sliding doors in the hall were replaced. The board was able to pass a vote to reduce a quorum for a meeting to 100. It had been 122. Jim and Joan Wilksmore hosted the Dec 9th coffee hour. 19 properties were sold during the year. Unit sales typically range from 12 to 24 a year. Recently more full time owners have moved to the park.

2018 - The street lights were refurbished with some new posts and new globes installed. Attractive acoustic ceiling tiles were installed in the ceiling of the hall to dampen the noise level. The proposed new Glen Creek housing project next to the country club was underway. Concerns about the impact resulted in several meetings with the county. The citrus inspector came to the park to evaluate the canker and greening disease destroying the trees.

2019 - The new SugarCreekResort.info web page was launched. It was a creation of John Eacott and Ginger Czubak. It will be the official site for the park. Herb Zuercher replaced Ken Wilson as President of the Association. Ken had several terms as president and served 12 years on the board. The Recreation club sold shirts and T shirts as a fund raiser. Ginger Czubak undertook to produce a Sugar Creek cook book that came out in 2020.

2020 - The season ended early for many as reports of a serious new virus sent people home, some for more than a year. Activities in the fall and following winter were disrupted. The park continued to move to contracting out more of the work. Pinch A Penny took over the pool maintenance. The pool fence was painted black. The dock was rebuilt with new posts. The BBQ pit, disused for a number of years, was filled in and palms planted in it. A Sugar Creek Resort cook book was created by Ginger Czubak. Leslie Pelkofer became an officer of the Recreation Club. Her father had served on the club for a number of years as well. Ken Fink of the Country Club led walking tours around Manatee county every week and had conducted 267 walks by the end of February. All that was required was to wear a name tag and be on time. Trips departed from the Country Club parking lot.

2021 - The U.S. and Canadian border was closed due to the Covid virus situation so Canadian owners and renters were unable to come to the park. The 20 year old wooden streets signs created by Dick Lawson have been replaced with new street signs. One Call Now service was installed to give every unit instant news about water shut off and other emergencies.

2022 - The history of the Sugar Creek Communities was published. Jennifer Wilcox became the first woman president of the board. In September hurricane Ian did some damage to units and trees. A sidewalk to Mixon's was completed. A new 7-11 is under construction across from Mixon's who announced they will cease to operate after 2023.

At the time of publication there were fewer than a dozen original owners remaining in the Sugar Creek Resort park. There were a number of units passed down within a family. When the park celebrated its 30th

anniversary in 2012 there were many more original owners. In 2022 of the 243 owners about 60 percent were not owners in 2012. There were 106 owners still in the park from 2012 some of whom had lost a mate during that time.

~~ *Back of the SCR hall and 3 shuffle courts about 1978-80* ~~

SUGAR CREEK COUNTRY CLUB and VILLAS
THE VILLAS STORY

In 1982 the ambitious projects of Bobby Whatley to develop the Country Club in 3 phases and the separate project of the smaller Villas looked good on paper. The Villas were to retain the aspects of a campground and the Country Club was to resemble a mobile home park yet retain the aspects of an RV park.

The 9 acres of the Villas may have been partly used as a plant nursery before being developed as a campground. The aerial photos show what might have been rows of something and the Sugar Creek Venture company indicated they were in the nursery business.

It appears that this project was too ambitious for Whatley and company and in 1984 the Bencin family owners of Rock Cove company and SCCC took over the project. The Sugar Creek Management Company wound up its business that year.

Sewers, water, streets and electricity were installed and Sugar Creek

Country Club was under way.

The Bencin purchase of the Villas was to keep it as a transient rental division for earning extra income for the SCCC project. They followed Whatley's plan until 1987 - 88 when it was decided to also sell Villas lots and end rental camping. As it was not part of the SCCC project proper, it was registered as a stand alone development with the state. In this way the Villas developed a separate identity for 16 years. So in 1987 Villa rentals ended. Rental rates are not known.

The Villas were a separate project on 9 acres. Because it was a smaller project it was soon sold out. The Villas had 35 units. A deal was made to use the adjacent facilities of the Country Club while maintaining its separate identity. The Villas property had two streets. Clubhouse Drive from the gates to the Country Club hall and sports area. This street had an easement for access to the SCCC club house and facilities. The other street was named Belinda Court after the wife of one of the new developers, Don Bencin. The only amenity of the Villas project was a small park picnic area between the Country Club hall and the tennis courts.

The Villas became functional in 1988 with twenty owners some of whom had 2 lots. It was not designated as a 55 and older park at the time.

Over the years the Villas organized themselves to deal with ongoing issues. The gates were a constant problem of needing repairs. Street lighting always needed repairs and making sure the park was always in a looking good condition was ongoing. Bill Campbell was always there to help keep the place presentable. A social committee sent out greeting and get well cards and members helped with projects at the SCCC club house.

The Villas, being a small project, still had an independent management operation. They used the services of AMI a management company to keep their books and administer their operation. A small park executive and the management company and deals with the Country Club made it work. The Villas maintained their independent status from 1988 until 2004 at which time a deal was struck to merge with the Country Club.

The two presidents of the respective parks were instrumental in bringing about the merger. Dick Anderson gives a very clear account of how this all came about.

"In 1992 we, Richard & Donna Anderson, Sugar Creek Villas #3, were invited by some friends, Bill and Dianne Campbell, to join them in a trip to a Park near Bradenton, FL during Easter vacation. Both families rented Lot #3 in Sugar Creek Villas, a small RV Park adjoining Sugar Creek Country Club. It was owned, at the time, by Harry Gastrich and his wife. We rented it for a week and got to know many of the folks in the two parks. Gastrichs also owned Lot #2 and were planning on putting a park model on that lot so their lot was for sale. Campbells owned Lot #4 right next to where we rented and were in the process of having a park model put on his lot.

They encouraged us to investigate purchasing Lot #3 and we made Harry an offer. My recollection is that we ended up buying the unit for $35,000, part of which Harry carried a mortgage for us. We paid that mortgage off in a short time and began making improvements to the unit. The original park model was 14' x 36' and was situated on a trapezoidal shaped lot with the back of the unit facing the park's tennis courts. We add on a 14' x 26' room to the street side and built a carport extending out toward the road. It has given us a very comfortable living quarters for the many years we have been staying here for the winters.

When we began staying for approximately 6 months, both my wife, Donna, and I became active in the functions of the park. I was asked to run for the Villas Board and ended up serving as its President from 1996 – 2004. Donna organized a group called the "Circle Committee" to undertake the beautification of the "green island" near the Clubhouse parking lot. Her group made many improvements including plantings, paths and generally improving the appearance of the "Circle". Along with others, I helped build an eight-sided platform which we hoped would be a gazebo. Unfortunately the gazebo never materialized due to construction rules but we still use the platform, which we refer to as the "Gazebo," to this date.

Along with my friend, Bill Campbell, we began to get a group of folks together to play guitar and sing at the Clubhouse. Around 2006, we officially called ourselves, the "Electric Corn Band". We have played together with as many as 12-14 local "musicians" periodically and enjoyed performing for folks from our park and the neighboring parks on Thursday evenings. A few of us still get together when conditions allow. Donna and I also put together, with the help of Wayne & Caroline Jacobs, a Sock Hop, with me acting as "Disc Jockey". We did that for several years. In addition we have helped organize a few of the dances held at the Clubhouse. Donna has been active and headed up the decorating committee for the Clubhouse for many years.

Back to the operation of the Villas and the events leading to the eventual merger of the Villas and the Country Club. Sugar Creek Country Club was originally formed as a member-owned and operated park when the members arranged to purchase the facilities from the developer, Bensin. The Villas was formed as a separate RV Park by the developer and acquired ownership in a similar manner. When we came to the Park, the villas had a lease agreement with the Counrty Club for the use and maintenance of the common grounds, clubhouse, tennis courts, swimming pools, shuffleboard courts, etc. Periodically the lease agreement between the Villas and the Country club was renegotiated. I was President of the Villas and Danny Finch was President of the Country Club and we were both good friends and golfing buddies. Dan even played and sang with the "Electric Corn Band" at times. In 2003 he and I began discussing the possibility for the merger of the two parks and over the period of a year the method and procedures for this to take place were developed. In 2004, paperwork was established and at member meetings both parks decided to merge with the Villa's residents buying in at the cost Country Club residents had originally paid including the amount of capital improvements. The merger became effective as of November 1, 2004. I went on to serve on the board of the combined parks and as Vice President for several years.

I consider myself fortunate to have been able to have become a part of what has been a very stable and reliable administration of both parks.

- Dick Anderson – 3/1/22"

In 1999 a committee of the Country Club board made a proposal of merger between the two parks. Access to the sport and social activities of the Country Club were accessible by a foot bridge or by car through the Villas road off of 33rd Street, a property owned by Sugar Creek Resort but shared by agreement with the Villas and Estates. No automobile access to the Country Club facilities was otherwise available. The Villas in turn had no recreational facilities other than a small park. The merger proposal in 1999 contained these proposed conditions.

1. Both parks would have to hold votes separately in which a majority voted in favor from each park.

2. The Villas would have to become a 55 and older park but current owners would be grandfathered.

3. Existing sheds and other building would be grandfathered but new structures would need to be approved by the Country Club.

4. Country Club rules and bylaws would apply to the Villas.

5. All merger legal costs would be shared equally.

6. All maintenance would be assumed by SCCC.

7. Each Villa lot owner would pay $1054 as a buy in to the mortgage as of January 2000.

8. SCCC would require a payment to their reserve equal to 9.6% of the total reserves of the SCCC (Sugar Creek Country Club) so as to gain equity for all parties. This would be $4,816 in total.

9. Villas pet section would not change.

This proposal was made by J. Johnson, Ed Stilson, and Bob Roy.

Some concern about the 2007 mortgage renewal by the SCCC and other financial matters caused the project to stall for some time. Coming up with the increasing buy in cost over each year kept the matter from being decided.

On March 6, 2002 a lease committee was formed by the Villas association to look into the lease between the SCCC and the Villas to explore the options as the expiration of the lease was on the horizon for 2007. Recommendations would be needed in due time. The lease committee was composed of Bill Campbell, Barb Bosse, Ken Wertz, Jerry Briggs and Charlotte Byrd.

The committee looked at the elements involved, including post box service, club house cleaning, cost of maintenance supervisor and maintenance, security, pool service, cleaning supplies, lift station, lawn mowing, pest control, energy costs, water and sewer, compactor costs, yard waste. The Villas paid from 4.2 to 8.4 percent of many of these costs with some exceptions. These items were formal agreements equal to about 9.6 percent of the SCCC budget. Without this agreement the Villas would be in an awkward position for essential services.

The committee considered important issues including;

1. revising the Prospectus respecting mandatory participation in the recreational facilities, opting out.

2. buying into which would be essentially joining the Country Club, or

3. having a yearly membership for Villas residents to use the recreation facilities.

However they would still be dependent upon the Country Club for shared utilities which at the time was about $69.00 per quarter. Which way should the future unfold?

By 2003 a concerted effort was made to go ahead with the "buy in" merger.

In April 2003 the Villas voted to become a 55 plus park. The Country Club at their annual meeting voted to approve a merger process. The proponents on February 16, 2004 undertook to meet with attorney Dan Loebeck who explained the procedure that was required to complete a merger including meeting state requirements. The committee consisted of park presidents Richard Anderson, Dan Finch, and Ken Wertz, Tom Roberts and Helen Koedoot.

When the Villas was formed, the prospectus included a proposed lease of the SCCC recreation facilities with the developer. The SCCC decided to buy the facilities outright and the Villas were obliged to pay the SCCC for their access for the remainder of the lease. So the Villas paid rent and their share of the expenses. This was for a fixed term that periodically was due to be renegotiated. A better arrangement was for the Villas to buy in to become full members of the SCCC, a full merger.

The proposed deal was similar to the nine points proposed in 1999 with some refinements.

These included along with full membership in the SCCC, turning over all maintenance and operational processes and expenses to the SCCC. The Villas would be guaranteed one advisory representative to the SCCC administration if one was not elected to the board. All Villas units would remain a pet section. Upon closing each unit would now have to pay $1,501.83 to gain equity with the SCCC owners. All assets of the Villas are to be turned over to the SCCC and the Sugar Creek Villas Corporation will be dissolved. The Villas owners would henceforth pay the same maintenance fee as the other park owners being $280.00 per quarter in 2004 which represented a reduction from the $371.00 then being paid. There would be no "opt out" provision if the vote was to pass.

These terms were worked out by both parks on Saturday October 25, 2003. The Villas at a special lot owners meeting on December 11, 2003 voted in principle to merge with the Country Club. The merger committee, Dick Anderson, Dean McDonald and Bill Campbell were all set to move ahead with the formal vote.

A special members meeting was called for Thursday April 22, 2004 at 1:00 pm. The business was to approve the plan of merger. The choice was to vote yes or no in favor of the merger. The Villas Board of Directors urged a yes vote.

The vote that day was 28 voting yes to the merger and none voting against.

The actual buy in costs turned out to be a little different that what was announced. As it turned out each unit had to pay $1,669.61 for their share. The Villas, which operated out of Sugar Creek Villas Association Inc. Lakewood Ranch Office 9031 Town Center Parkway, Bradenton, was to wind up its affairs on November 1st, 2004 and all the financial tidying up had to be dealt with by then.

On November 1st, 2004 the Sugar Creek Country Club and Villas became a new organization.

Dick and Donna Anderson went on to be active leaders in the new organization. As Dick said in his introduction letter to be a candidate for the board " ... *I was asked to run for the Villas Board of Dir. I have served on that board until the recent merger with the Country Club for four years as secretary treasurer and for the past four years as president....* "

Dick went on to explain about their leadership with the golf league, dance committee, Circle Park, and being part of the Electric Corn Band. Through the efforts of people like Dick the merged parks quickly became a cohesive functioning organization.

Signing of the merger papers 2004 Bill Campbell, Richard Anderson, Dan Finch, Helen Koedoot, Carolyn Gordon, Bob Roy. (Not in order)

~~~~~~~~~~ *From Prospectus Brochure 1985* ~~~~~~~~~~

SUGARCREEK Country Club

3333 - 26th AVENUE EAST
BRADENTON, FLORIDA 33508
(813) 748-4451

OFFERING

CLUBHOUSE FEATURING:
- MENS & LADIES SAUNAS
- MENS & LADIES LOCKER ROOMS
- GAME ROOM
- EXERCISE ROOM
- WORKSHOP
- OFFICES

SWIMMING POOL
JACUZZI
TENNIS COURTS
BOATDOCKS WITH DIRECT ACCESS TO THE GULF OF MEXICO
GOLF (minutes away)

All the beauty and splendor of the Florida outdoors and within minutes of one of Florida's largest shopping malls.

The Sugar Creek Country Club

"The most luxurious adult RV community on the west coast of Florida" it said on the back of this post card from 1985.

Earlier the opening story of the Country Club or SCCC laid the foundations of Bobby Whatley's project. For the next part of the development project new owners came on the scene. The reasons for this change involved the cost of installing all the infrastructure needed and was beyond what Whatley could afford and it was an opportunity for him to cash in his assets and walk away as he had 3 girls to send to college.

Whatley's partner company, Sugar Creek Venture, was created in the early spring of 1981 as a co-op campground and sales group which was also in the nursery and related businesses. The company was composed of Bobby N. Whatley holding 35% of the shares, Thomas Lain, Lorraine Huntzinger (lot 8 and 102 SCR), Carlos Joslin each holding 10% and Lila Pearson, Colin Jackson, T.G. Wells, Venice Investments, Jay Joslin each with 5%. Several others held 2.5% each. It was this company that was involved with the creation of SCCC. On June 4th, 1981 This company borrowed $25,000 to buy vacant land adjacent to Sugar Creek Resort and Estates from Harold Karp and John Kazanjian. This land was bought to become SCCC and the Villas. Subsequently Sugar Creek Venture borrowed a great deal more money to launch the project.

The trail of documents go back to 1981 with a loan from the Ellis First National Bank. This $750,000 loan and a subsequent second mortgage of $ 75,000 resulted in a debt of $825,000 that Sugar Creek Venture had created over the SCCC project. The interest was an extreme 18.5% per annum as at the 17th day of July 1981 but that was renegotiated to 2% above prime. This company was controlled by Whatley and the general manager was Lorraine Hunzinger. They had borrowed a lot of money in a costly mortgage market to move the project ahead or was it to sell it off quickly and make some money? Whatever the reasons Whatley's Sugar Creek Country Club ownership barely lasted 2 years before being sold to Rock Cove.

Rock Cove was a Punta Gorda company controlled by the Bencin family. The Rock Cove Inc. project was owned by Don and Charles Bencin and was incorporated in 1982 and began operations in 1983.

Don Bencin 1938-2000 was from the Cleveland Ohio area and became an engineer. He worked for B.F. Goodrich before founding ENMCO which had factories in Ohio. He and his wife Belinda sold the company in 1982 and he had the wealth to join with his older brother Charles, 1929 -2003 a real estate person to form Rock Cove to purchase the Sugar Creek land.

Negotiations with Sugar Creek Venture took place over several months culminating with the sale of land south of the Braden River, east of Sugarhouse Creek and south of Glen Creek less the south 33 ft. on March 4th 1983. The liabilities of Sugar Creek Venture were assumed and Bobby N. Whatley was paid, under a complex formula based on lot sales, the sum total of $175 000 on Nov 1, 1984. At about this time Whatley closed up his Sugar Creek Management Company.

On the 23rd of November 1983 Rock Cove, with the agreement of Sugar Creek Venture, the mortgage holder, consented to the documents to create the co-operative and the articles of incorporation as well as the bylaws for Sugar Creek Country Club Travel Trailer Park Association Inc.

The new company began selling lots. The first Lot #1011 was sold the 7th of August 1984. The next lot #1023 sold 12th of September, followed by #1004 also in September then in November #1077, #1003 and in December #1081. Beginning in the new year of 1985 numerous sales were completed. This was phase one of three phases.

Thus the project was left in new hands and the projects proceeded more or less according to the original plan. Charles Bencin was president and his brother Don was vice president. Don's wife, Belinda, was also a vice president. The company was part of the Recreational Vehicle Parks and Recreational Camps Industry. The original company is no longer active but there is/was the Sugar Creek RV and Boat Storage at 3332 26th Ave East, Bradenton. The SCCC address is 3333.

Surprisingly, when I began this book, I had no idea that Whatley did not complete the SCCC project and people in SCCC and the Villas had never heard of Whatley.

By 1987 SCCC was becoming known as a destination and the local shopping guide wrote up a nice article about the park just as a new phase of the project was opening up for sale. The article dated March 25th 1987 mentioned that 170 lots had been completed and 184 new lots were just coming up for sale. These lots were typically 40 ft wide and 69 feet 9 inches deep.

The article began by telling about the different lifestyle choices available to those coming to Florida and went on to tell about SCCC.

"*Sugar Creek Country Club R.V Park is an ideal place to begin the search. It is ideal in that for many the search will end there as well. The physical setting is idyllic. The benefits of the clubhouse, pool, and other types of facilities are numerous. The price is right. The people who come there make life interesting and fun....*"

The article went on to describe the park in more detail and concluded with a recommendation to drive by, sample the atmosphere and tour the models available for sale.

The evolution and operating nature of the SCCC turned out differently than the other two parks which each had a board and an influential recreation group. It also had not evolved out of campers who bought lots and as mentioned earlier had been set up to resemble a mobile home park and still remain an RV park. The other two parks, especially the Resort, had distinct elements of their camping origin.

In 1997 George Howland wrote a brief history of the Sugar Creek Country Club. That is reproduced here:

Our Board of Directors: a Brief History

Development of our park began back in the early 1980's with the first lot being sold in late 1985. At that time our Board of Directors consisted of the developers, Rock Cove Inc. and a unit owner appointee named Joe Schmidt of lot #1061. Thereafter Harold Fisher of lot #1079 was elected by us to fill the minority position on the board.

While the principals of Rock Cove Inc., the Bencin brothers, by name were "hail fellows" and quite a social pair; they were, after all, serious businessmen with the goal of profit uppermost on their list of priorities! As lots were sold the problems normally attributed to growth, multiplied and required some very difficult negotiations on the part of Harold Fisher to maintain a beneficial relationship between two parties historically at odds with one another. Lot owners and developers, quite simply, have opposite interests and desires. Many lot owners wishes and/or requests, as echoed by our advisory committee, were agreed to by the developer at the urging of Harold in his minority position on the board, but many were not. As time went by, many problems were resolved but some remained and the most serious of which grew to such proportions that an explanation must be offered so that the extreme difficulties in running our park during this time can best be understood.

We had a lot owner who started off apparently, as a well intentioned "do-gooder" but he became the most destructive and horrendous activist in the annals of the State Department of Business Regulation, Division of Condos and Co-ops. This individual, guided by what has been described as a "pathological drive" to enforce regulations to his specific ideals, created for the developer and our early boards of directors, an unending series of problems and demands that, until his eventual "ouster" from the park, resulted in our expenditure of moneys in the area of seventy five thousand dollars in legal fees dealing with his outrageous conduct. In addition to the expense, the overall fear, disgust and unhappiness his actions undoubtedly created. Those of us who were charged with operating the park, were driven to "near madness" with frustration as fending him off became a near full time job! It took our "winning" a massive arbitration action, a counter-law suit against this person and finally some very active "picketing" of his residence and a buy-out to rid ourselves of this social malignancy. Had only his energies been expended in a positive direction how much more peace of mind and enjoyment of life we'd have shared. Thank God we at last saw an end to this most pitiful situation. (See "Park's Nightmare" pp 152-154)

After "turn-over" by the developer back in May of 1991, we now had a two person majority on the board with the election of Russ Helmer of lot #1096 and George Howland of lot #1300. Don Bencin of Rock Cove continued to serve in the minority slot until all lots were sold and he was then replaced by Merle Richie of lot #1081. This earliest of full membership boards was soon to be expanded to include the following individuals: Ben Pfeiffer #1302, Bill Roy #1136, Betty Schlough #1028 and Elmer Russell #1029.

This group now dealt with the normal problems inherent in a "fledgling" co-operative administration, no longer able to look to the developer for guidance, good or bad. This earliest board handled the day to day operation of the park.

Some of the earlier problems and projects that needed attention (in addition to the "activist" grief mentioned earlier) that might be of interest were the upgrading of our sewer system which is of obvious importance and the building of our maintenance and wood shop edifice. A serious dispute known as the McClure property line, east of us, was inherited from the developer, who simply avoided the problem time and time again and refused to take action on our behalf as he was able to "hide behind" his title insurance program. His inaction left us with legal fees in the area of eighty five hundred dollars spent to no avail. We were under the impression that an additional twenty foot border was on our property along this entire 1800 foot line. Face to face meetings with Mr. McClure and the Director of the County Zoning and Development Department did not resolve this mess but we were quite disappointed to learn that proper title to this land was held since 1939 by McClure. Our developer, lawyer and surveyors were either misguided, misinformed, lazy or incompetent, but in any event, records were corrected and the fence properly reinstalled and planted.

Our most important long term decision was whether or not we should recommend to our lot owners, the purchase of our leased recreation area. This would be an expensive and long range commitment. We had to negotiate with the developer and, surprisingly, with several lot owners before we took the plunge. Most agree now that it was the right thing to do.

Our next Board of Directors, headed up by Russ Helmer, consisted of the following: Rosemary Aumaugher # 1059. Joan Beckley #1080, Ken Moore # 1063, Howard Millard # 1070, Bill Roy and George Howland again. Most of the accomplishments mentioned herein actually "overlap" the tenure of our various boards so that "historical" dating may be somewhat vague.

For 1994 and 1995 our boards were headed by Joan Beckley and she was assisted by Howard Brouwer # 1085. Ed Stilson #1337 and Carolyn Gordon #1334 the first year and then Jerry Johnson #1339 and Augie Turnes #1167 came on board.

These good people continued to operate the park and refine our many procedures including the imposition of computerized accounting! It was under the "watch" of this Board the property purchase and final expulsion of our aforementioned activist took place. How many meetings were held? How many visits to Tampa to the "division" were made, how much paperwork, lawyers time and general aggravation was suffered by this Board on so nasty a problem? You stuck with it to the end and we do thank you and those others involved most sincerely!

We come now to the present Board that was actually formed last year in 1996, chaired by Ed Stilson and is composed of the following individuals. George Leach, # 1179, Helen O'Brien # 1174, John Pettinger #1027, along with Howard Brouwer, Jerry Jophnson and Augie Tuenes who stayed aboard. There was one change though for 1997 where in Rosemary Aumaugher returned to serve as treasurer, replacing Jerry Johnson who resigned to serve as a financial consultant to our Association.

Along with the continued excellent operation of our park from an administrative and financial point of view, this board was successful in the complete re-paving of our streets east of the creek.

Attention to detail along with very watchful eyes must be the guiding theme of these volunteer groups of individuals because when one looks back most carefully we find that while our park is "humming along" in good fashion, our fees have come from outside, or nondiscretionary influences! The fact that we at Sugar Creek Country Club enjoy so very much for so little in dollars speaks volumes for the effort and devotion put forth by those serving us so well.

Compiled by George Howland. 1997

The above document is to be found in the collection of photo books in the SCCC library.

~~~ 1984 - 1986 Belinda, Don, and Charles Bencin ~~~

1984 - First lots were sold in SCCC and the last lots were sold in SCR.

1985 - A board was created by the developers and Joe Schmidt an owner was appointed by the board to represent owners. On November 8, 1985 over half of the first 100 lots, lots 1001 to 1105 had been sold. The price of an interior lot was $12,900, while corner, water front and exterior were more.

Board 1988 to 1991 Bencin brothers and Harold Fisher

1986 - Construction of large pool.

1988 - there were now 131 owners. Lot prices on the water ranged from $15,900 to $19,500, corner lots were $16,900 and east side lots $15,900 the 63.5 x 39.5. Interior lots had been raised by $1,000 to $13,900. The Board members were developers Charles and Don Bencin and Harold Fisher was elected by the owners.

An advisory council chaired by Tom Dale, Vice Del Adams, Secretary Helen DeBack, Treasurer Marg Miller and 4 members Walter Bouchard, Merle Richie, Wallace Miller, John Crotty was created.

1989 - By 1990 an Activities Committee had been created. An early draft suggested the name, "Sugar Creek Country Club Recreation and Social Organization". Its purpose was stated as follows: "To provide and encourage recreation and social opportunities for the residents and guests of Sugar Creek Country Club and the Villas and assist in the maintenance of the recreational facilities subject to the approval of the Board of Dir."

1990 - The Advisory Council continued with expanded duties.

1991 - The Board of Directors elected George Howland president. He was also the treasurer. The vice president and secretary was Russell Helmer and Don Bencin represented the owners. In addition there was an Operating Board with a chair and a number of assistants. The developer turned over the park to the owners.

1992 - The owners became distinct from the Board and the Executive Committee. George Howland was the president and Russell Helmer vice president. George Howland was also chair of the Executive Committee which had 3 officers and 18 sub committees to run the park.

The creation of a new community comes with all sorts of organization issues and a need for different amenities. One amenity which became popular was the creation of a wood work shop. Leadership for this was by Paul Blankenship who organized and set up the shop.

The following document covers the details about how the SCCC woodwork shop came into being in 1992 and it includes some of the problems all community run shops run into.

1-19-92
ROUGH Draft: **SCCC Wood Working Shop Organization:**

Discuss decision to formally organize the shop into a club.
Result of discussion:
Select name for club, if club is to be formed.
Recommend club Officers by office name not personnel.
Discuss qualifications for membership, dues, etc.
Discuss method for control of use of equipment, viz. regarding knowledge of equipment and safety practices.
Discuss funding and line of responsibility for handling funds.
Set up guidelines for what the shop is to be used for regarding magnitude or size of projects to be done in the shop, and if necessary, method for controlling the shop scheduling, supervision of the shop, line of authority in the shop, etc.

Discuss officers further with respect to periodic meetings, election of officers and method of determining quorum for establishing rules and regulations.

Determine type of documentation needed to comply with legal and acceptable procedures as required by the Association, and the dissemination of same.

Discuss other pertinent subjects such as shop signs, liability, etc.
The above thoughts are all that come to my mind at this time and I'm sure that they are not all inclusive, however they are a start and with other input I think we can work out a good shop, small as it is, and grow with it as time goes on. Following are some of my thoughts regarding the above subjects, and in no way would I want to imply that they are "set in concrete" in my mind as I believe to hang meat on and to perhaps stimulate discussion from others. in consensus in all respects. These thoughts are just a skeleton.
So, here goes:
I think that we should organize the shop into a club, with officers and delegated responsibility. I think we should determine membership by payment of token dues and I also believe that members should demonstrate a capability of understanding and practicing safe and proper use of the tools. This should not be taken for granted and those who do have satisfactory experience should review this with them thru actual

demonstration of the equipment. If this offends the person involved to the extent that he will not cooperate and comply, then I think membership and/or use of the equipment should be denied. As I stated once before, the term "wood worker" is very generic as most everyone has performed some kind of wood work during their lifetime .This is not sufficient criteria to permit them to use this shop unless they have had specific experience or training with the tools they are about to use. In our particular case, our principal tool is the multi-purpose tool known as a Shopsmith. Because it is five tools built into one, it requires a specific set-up for each function and therefore this requires knowledge of how to set up these different modes. Individual tools require much less knowledge. To close out this subject I will cite an example. A gentleman came into the shop to do a job and he was asked if he knew how to use the tools and he replied that he had worked in a furniture plant for 32 years and he thought he could handle everything. This job involved the use of the Shopsmith and I readily observed that he was unfamiliar with the tool and I asked him in a very friendly way if he had ever used this type machine. He said that he had not so I helped him with his job explaining everything I did as we went along. He was very receptive to the instruction; he got his job done and he at least learned how to operate the machine for that one set-up.

~~~~~~~~~ *Storage and workshop 1992* ~~~~~~~~~~

Regarding funds for the shop, I think we should have the proceeds from the sale of aluminum cans allocated directly to the shop to cover operating expenses. I think the club officers should have complete control of the money, to be spent as they see fit, with complete accountability, audit wise. The club treasurer would handle this responsibility. Other fund raising projects should be considered as apropos and all club rules and activities should conform to Association rules and regulations, as the club would not be completely autonomous, however it should not be constrained unnecessarily.

I think that the shop should be primarily considered as a hobby type shop, limited mostly to small projects which can be turned out handily in the small area which we have. Large projects such as furniture building, etc. should be limited, except for work for the Association. We have the capability to perform most any type woodworking job and our first priority should always be for the Association. Because of the small shop area, only about three people can safely and efficiently work in there at one time, however with the use of a little common judgement and cooperation among everyone this should be no problem.

A good bit of our work in the shop thus far has been in the area of people who have only a single job to do or have done, and I expect that this continue to be the case. In the.past we have stopped whatever we were doing and done the job or helped them do it. In-as-much as a non-member will not be able to use the tools a member will do it for them and we will accept whatever donation they wish to make as compensation. We will lend the power of suggestion to them by placement of a sign and receptacle in good view. Club members will have access to the shop at all times thru lock control.

It is estimated at this time we have 25 to 30 dollars in cans to be sold. With membership dues and residuals from raffled projects this would give us a start and enable us to buy some much needed shop supplies. One cannot expect everything to be idealistic at the beginning, or ever, however with cooperation and understanding from everyone, we can make it work and I think that having a shop, even as small as it is, is a good adjunct to the Park. This view has been expressed by many park residents. Even with non-members and residents who have no interest in woodworking, it is good to know that if they ever had the need for even a small woodworking job, they can get it done right here at home at virtually no cost. While I am on this subject I would require the person who wants a job done, or who is doing it themselves, furnish the materials needed. This would apply to materials of significant cost only, certainly not miscellaneous items which we would have around the shop. Follow up six months later.

The shop has only been operating for about six months and we have made out pretty good. We have done three significant jobs for the Association and will start another one soon. Most of the other activity has been with John, Merriel and myself, and while we involve ourselves with small projects the main objective was to keep the shop open to advertise its existence; help or do jobs for others, and organize the shop. We have had very few problems, however to illustrate the need for tool use monitoring, just last week John and I found the bandsaw guides destroyed thru mis-use and fortunately John was able to make new ones. These are metal components and are not available as replaceable parts due to the age of the saw. The point here is that everyone who uses this saw should know how to check the guides and adjust them, if needed, before proceeding. This is especially imperative if a blade size is changed. Also, our 6 inch belt sander was found to be out of belt adjustment causing the belt to cut into the aluminum frame, which would ultimately destroy this very valuable tool. So, it is up to those of who know these machines to keep an eye on them and advise and instruct those who do not know these procedures to keep our tools operable. We cannot afford to buy new tools. Our visit to Trailer Estates was very profitable as they have a role model shop in my opinion, however, they probably started out just like we are doing, so with everyone pulling in the same direction maybe some day we will be equally as proud. If we will just try to view our problems objectively, looking at both sides of the issues, not being opinionated or controversial, we can succeed.

As stated before the above commentary is solely my own and certainly subject to any and all other thoughts, and I am sure I have not covered all aspects. I would not want one to think that we are over reacting to the subject or making "too big a deal" out of it, but it pays to think about all the parameters as it is easier to pare them down if they are not applicable than it is to implement them later.

Now, let's have a meeting and "get on with it".

Sincerely, Paul Blankenship Lot 1134

The New Saw-Dust work shop. 1992

Later wood shop users see how Paul's efforts have been realized and become important to the park. There is a follow up later in the book.

1993 - the park operation consolidated into one organization with many sub committees. SCCC was now totally in the hands of the owners.

1994 - Difficulties with owner Calvin Garing caused residents to launch a protest that was reported in the local newspaper in December 1994. Garing eventually left the park after some considerable legal confrontation.

Park's 'nightmare' over as man leaves

ANNETTE GILLESPIE Feb-1995
Herald Staff Writer

A man who was picketed by his neighbors and described in a lawsuit as a "one man neighborhood nightmare" has moved out of his home.

Calvin Garing became known in the community for his numerous complaints about the management of Sugar Creek Country Club Travel Trailer Park, which frustrated many of the park residents.

Despite that, Garing had planned to spend his retirement there.

He and his wife, Dorothy, lived at the park off 26th Avenue East since 1987. The Garings could not be reached Thursday; their telephone number was disconnected.

Last April, more than 390 residents filed a class-action lawsuit against Garing to seek a temporary and permanent injunction to prevent him from harassing them and trespassing on their properties. His next-door neighbor and others recently began picketing in front of his home.

The attorney representing the residents, Robert Watrous of Sarasota, said the case will be dismissed when he receives written confirmation about the closing on Garing's house.

The association's attorney, Mark Hanson of Sarasota, said a lawsuit Garing filed against the association last year also will be dismissed.

"The case has been resolved to mutual satisfaction of both parties," Hanson said. However, he said he could not discuss the legal agreement or confirm whether the association bought Garing's property from him.

Joan Beckley, president of the association, also declined comment.

George Howland, 65, a Sugar Creek resident, declined to talk about the legal agreement, but described the attitude in the park as "joyous" shortly before a block party Thursday.

"We hope it's ancient history in our park. It finally came to an end."

Elmer Russell, activities director, submitted his report outlining the list of dances, shows including the variety show, Las Vegas Night, pot lucks, pancake breakfasts, and weekly bingo. With the money that was made two new shuffle courts and benches were built. A pool table and gym and kitchen equipment were purchased. Marge Boyle did the calendar, sold tickets and helped in other ways.

1995 - Over the years changes have been made to the clubhouse but the dates in which they occurred are often forgotten. The early pictures show a very different building. Inside a storage room near the kitchen is a "trapdoor" at the ceiling. From there one can view the upper area which was to become a "restaurant". Where the current ladies' restroom and a storage room are off the exercise room, there were once sauna rooms for women and men.

Originally the mail room was only accessible from an outside door. A small air conditioner presently is inserted in that closed door adjacent to the Dutch door entrance accessible from the library/pool room area.

1996 -

Gerritt & Ruth Koedoot He was well known as pastor for the Sunday church services from 2001 to 2017.

~~~~~~~~~ *The Club house as it was in the first years* ~~~~~~~~~

1997 - Streets paved in entire park.

1998 - "The Circle". A portion of the Villas was an area designated as a picnic area. It had some tables but as it was between the SCCC tennis courts and the SCCC club house it became a neglected common area. Donna Anderson one of the founders of the "Circle Committee" became interested in this patch of ground and tells the story of what became of it.

"When we first came to Sugar Creek, the "Circle" had been neglected and many weeds had grown up! The Campbell's, our neighbors, also were interested in improving the appearance of this area. We got permission to work in the circle.

I remember Gene Gordon, the maintenance supervisor, coming out to the circle while the four of us were working and making sure we had permission to be there. After all, we were from the "Villas".

We had a regular clean-up day. We had about six or seven that came out to rake and do odd jobs. We asked for plants to be donated and made use of donated edging and other garden decorations. After Christmas, the "Circle" turned red with Poinsettias .

Tom Roberts was President of the Country Club Board about this time. I think the board helped financially in the building of the octagonal platform that was to become the base of a "Gazebo". Due to county code regulations, the upper part of the "Gazebo" structure was never able to be completed.

As we thought of putting benches on the "Gazebo" platform and around the circle, people wanted to donate a bench in memory of a loved one, but that was discouraged. Anne, our former post office mail lady had passed away, so "we" put a new "mailbox" out on the edge of the circle with her name on it. It did not say, "In Memory Of", but of course it was implied. It upset the Board and a few others so it was taken down. The Board did not want the "Circle" to become a "memorial" park.

During this time, we created paths through the "Circle" as well as a sprinkling system installed by Bill Campbell. A few years passed and another incident occurred. Terry Daly, a resident of the Country Club, without permission, had a large tree planted in the "Circle", and near it, placed a memorial plaque for her husband. She was told by the board that she could leave the tree but had to remove the plaque. She removed both.

The committee sort of lost interest at that point and could never decide upon the kind of ground covering (grass, shells, etc.). During the summer, the Board hired a professional landscaper to come in and remove all the various flowers, especially those with thorns. All the edging, and the cement picnic table placed there earlier, were removed. Grass was planted but most of the paths were left intact. It is very clean looking now and taken care of by our groundskeeper.

It is still decorated for Christmas which was first done by the "Circle

Committee" when the Activities Committee gave us $200 to purchase some lights and decorations."

1999 - The annual farewell party continued as a highlight of the year.

Sugar Creek Country Club & Villas
Farewell Party
Tuesday, March 24th
Music by Wayne's World 1 - 4:00 PM
Dinner, 4:15 at Clubhouse (Catered by Recipe Box)
$10.00 per person donation*

M·E·N·U
Stuffed Chicken Breast
Potatoes & Vegetables
Rolls & Butter
Dessert & Coffee

*Activities Fund is donating $2 per person + the

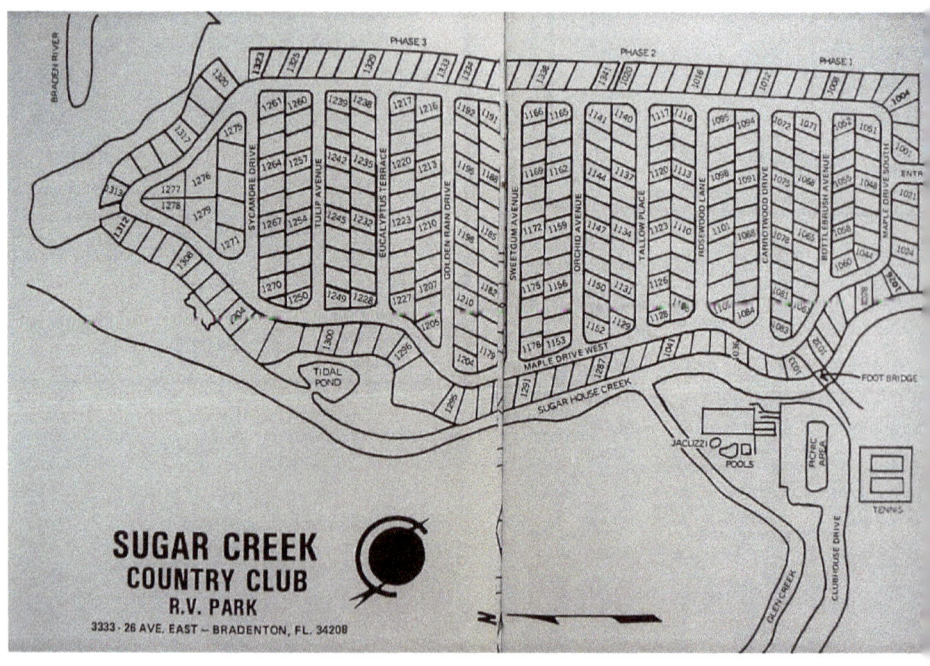

SUGAR CREEK COUNTRY CLUB R.V. PARK
3333 - 26 AVE. EAST – BRADENTON, FL. 34208

2000 - New steps on club house

2001 - Ken Fink begins his popular "walks". His experience in being a member of the Cleveland Hiking Club served as his inspiration to begin his walks.

On December 5, 2001, after Ken and Clarice Fink first moved into their mobile home in the Sugar Creek Country Club, Ken led the first of "Weekly Walks" (aka "Out-of-the-Park-Walks") that continued each season up to the 271st walk on February 3, 2021. Each season the walks usually began at the end of November and continued until mid-March when residents began returning north and the weather became too uncomfortable. For that first walk twenty-five residents from the Country Club and Resort met at the Country Club parking lot and car pooled to the boat launch at the Braden River near Manatee Avenue and walked on streets near the Braden River and then the streets in Braden River Park.

Ken modeled the walks after those of the Cleveland Hiking Club, founded in 1919, that continues strong today with volunteer leaders for usually six hikes every day in the Cleveland, Ohio area and volunteers organize and lead multi-day hiking excursions in the United States, Canada, and beyond.

Regarding the Sugar Creek walks, Ken announced them at coffee hours, in newsletters, in E-mails, and through Kris Tuttle, the Resort secretary. Walks were any day of the week and at any time including evening. Residents and their guests did not have to register for the walks but were just to arrive at the SCCC parking lot at the designated time. They were encouraged to wear name tags, even if their name was written on masking tape. Fortunately, in all the driving to and from destinations, there were no vehicle accidents. In all the walks, the only injury occurred when one walker slipped at the edge of the Manatee River in Rye Preserve. He then drove to Lakewood Ranch Urgent Care for the injury to his nose.

For the 271 weekly walks, participants in each walk were as few as 5 to as many as 64. The average number was 25 participants per walk. Following are some destinations of previous walks:

Beach: Anna Maria Island (north), Coquina Bay Walk, Greer Island, Palmetto Estuary, Sarasota Rec Trail.
Christmas Lights: Downtown Bradenton, Downtown Palmetto, Grace Baptist Church, Inlets Gas Lights, Palma Sola, Peridia, River Walk.
Neighborhoods: Cortez Village, Downtown Palmetto, Downtown Sarasota, Downtown Venice, Fogartyville, Historic Manatee, Lakewood Ranch, Longboat Key (North), Peridia, Pinecraft Amish, Village of the Arts.
Parks: Celery Fields, Conservatory, Durante, Emerson Point Preserve, Fort De Soto and Skyway Bridge, Heron's Nest, Manatee Viewing Center, Myakka River, Oscar Scherer, Rothenbach, Robinson Preserve, Rye Preserve, Weedon Island.
Tours: Manatee Historic Village, Pirate City.

Due to the impact of Covid in 2020, Ken halted the walks. The clubhouses were closed, most activities stopped, and Canadians could not return while others chose not to return. Ken has extensive files on his computer and printed material regarding past walks. With the lessening of Covid and the recent influx of new residents into the Sugar Creek communities, the weekly walks may resume.

2002 - tai chi classes were organized and a new roof was completed on the club house during 2001.

Bob Roy arranged seventeen cruises from 2001 until 2011. Then Tom and Joyce Miller arranged a tour each year until 2022. Their 2020 cruise departed Fort Lauderdale but had to return two days later due to the covid pandemic. The cruises included trips to Alaska, Hawaii, Panama Canal, Antigua, Barbados, St. Maarten, St. Thomas, St. Mark, St. John, St. Luke, Nassau, Aruba, Trinidad, Jamaica, and Granada.

Clarice and Ken Fink arranged motorcoach tours to Florida casinos including Hard Rock Tampa, Seminole Immokalee, Cape Canaveral ship, East Coast (Isle of Capri, Coconut Creek, Hard Rock Hollywood, Gulfstream).

Liz & Dick Henrich together with Margaret and Gordon Beaulieu arranged "Entertainment Outside" from 2008 to 2019. Barbara Wilkomm did it in 2019 but not since the Covid pandemic.

2003 - The interior of the club house was painted white.
2004 - merger with Villas

Signing of the Merger of Villas and Country Club
2004
Bill Campbell-Richard Anderson-Dan Finch-Helen Koedoot
Carolyn Gordon- Bob Roy

2005 -

2006 -

2007 - All roads were totally reconstructed. At a special meeting on March 27, 2007 SCCC and Villas met with representatives from Ajax Paving Industries. Questions and answers were fielded and it was finally decided to go ahead with the project. The general consensus was for the road work to be paid by a special assessment instead of borrowing and paying interest. Subsequently it was approved to spend $ 171,274.80 with an additional $5,000 for drains and extras. $34,000 of that was drawn from the reserves leaving $142,274 to be met by the owners. Each lot had a share of $390. This was passed on March 27th and owners had until May 30th to meet the assessment.

2008 -

2009 - In two stages the shuffle courts were provided new covers this year and in 2013.

2010-

2011 - During the New Year's Eve Dance (January 1, 2011), Sugarhouse Creek flowed over the pedestrian bridge while some rainwater entered from the many clubhouse sliding doors. The sliding doors were not for entering or exiting the clubhouse but only to allow exterior air to enter when opened. Among the options not chosen to solve the problem were re-caulking to seal leaks, replacing all the sliding doors, removing all the sliding doors and installing solid walls, and installing lower walls with fixed picture windows above them. The option chosen was installing six three-foot high sliding glass windows, each starting four feet above the floor. After the windows were installed, a new floor was also installed.

2012 - Got Talent show.

The propane supply costs for energy for the pools and laundry became a matter of concern. Carl Beatty was involved with the negotiations and the company representative proved difficult to deal with.

Carl writes of what happened next.

"In 2012 I was negotiating with the current propane supplier regarding our next year supply price for the pools and laundromat. The sales manager informed me because the underground tanks were their rentals, the price was not negotiable. I called his bluff and stopped all deliveries. Several weeks later he called me and asked why we were not taking deliveries of propane. He told me I was not allowed to have other suppliers fill their tanks. I informed him we were running the tanks empty and would be installing our own. He said yes, I bet you are!! He sent one of their service technicians over to check the fuel level in our tanks.

Well, he bet wrong and the Board did buy and install our own 2000 gal. tank in the pool area. I then negotiated a three-year supply agreement with a new supplier at a price that saved the park more then the price of the new tank and installation.

We are now free to purchase our propane from what ever supplier gives us the best price.

It was with great pleasure that I called the sales manager and informed him he had 3 days to pick up his rental tanks in our parking lot, or if not, I would send them for scrap.

As a footnote: shortly after the tank installation and everything was back up and running smoothly, I received a visit from the original supplier's regional sales manager. He asked me why I had terminated our supply contract with them. I told him I did not like being threatened and his sales manager refused to negotiate. After asking me to reconsider and saying he could meet or beat the best price or I could get elsewhere. I told him it was too late. I had a three-year deal, and a bad taste from dealing with his staff. It was then that he told me that the loss of our contract and the removal of the underground tanks was the final broken straw in the sales manager's employment with his company. Not the outcome I was looking for, but then he did call my bluff, didn't he?"

Some Pool facts for SCCC and Villas. The large Pool holds 51,757 gals. That circulates at 269 gpm flow rate. The Kidney Pool aka Canadian pool which is called that because it is not heated holds 33,196 gals and circulates at 92 gpm. The Spa holds 480 gals. and circulates at 40 gpm and is heated to a temperature of approx. 102 F.

2013 - In 2013 after the exterior of the clubhouse was done, a complete new kitchen was done. As a result, the entrance to the men's room was closed. Now the entrance to the men's room is past the library/pool room and off the exercise room.

One account, difficult to verify, concerns a fire that could have destroyed the clubhouse. On a Sunday morning prior to the weekly Sunday church service, the fire department was called after extensive smoke was noticed coming from the side of the clubhouse close to the hot tub. It is believed that the fire started in the room with the electrical equipment for the hot tub.

2014 - Sunday February 2nd - OFFICIAL REPORT *"The Florida Highway Patrol says a white 2009 Chevy Tahoe SUV backed from a parking space at Sugar Creek Country Club at 3333 26th Ave. E. in Bradenton, FL. and killed three pedestrians and left four seriously injured, with the vehicle ending submerged in a canal.*

Dead are pedestrians Margaret Vanderlaan age 72, Wilhemina Paul age 70, and Johanna Dijkhoff age 80, all of Bradenton. Seriously injured were Nelly Depooter age 67 of Ontario, Canada, Nellie Alice Vlasma age 75 of Bradenton, Michael Claus age 79 of Bradenton, and Fred Eringa age 89 of Bradenton.

A Chevy Tahoe, driven by 79-year old Doreen E. Landstra of Palmetto, Fl. pulled forward and needed more room to clear another parked vehicle said a FHP report and the SUV began backing eastbound again. In doing so, the rear struck seven pedestrians who were standing in the parking lot behind the vehicle. It continued to travel east over a curb before colliding with small trees and then entered a canal where it came to final rest facing west partially submerged said Trooper Keil Nanan and homicide investigator Cpl. Ronnie Highsmith."

2015 -

2016 - plans were made to add new gym equipment to the exercise room which was done in 2017

2017 - Comments from Carl Beatty

In 2016 after many years of building and managing the woodshop John Cronin decided to retire. He approached Bob Aumaugher and myself Carl Beatty to take over from him. We agreed to take over management of the shop starting in the Fall of 2017.

In 2017 the shop had approximately 40-50 members, and membership dues were $10 per year. We quickly realized how much time and effort John and his team of helpers (Dave Wingo, Norm Ferguson, John Klinginsmith) put in looking after the shop. I am sure there were others who helped, this is the gang I knew best. At present the management team consist of Carl Beatty, Dennis Finch, Dennis Custer, Randy Stone. Helping with machine maintenance and construction are members Don Richards and Don Eash.

In the last five years shop upgrades included a new and expanded dust collection system. The installation of LED lights through out the whole shop. The rewiring of several machines for safety reasons. Building a new bench system for the Miter saws. Purchase and installation of two new Air Compressor systems, two used but larger, improved wood lathes. Up graded roof, steel sheet instead of shingles.

In 2018, I instated a new policy allowing for the sign out and borrowing of power tools from the shop for a period of up to four days. This has proven very popular with the residents doing home renovations.

The woodshop has always been involved with improvement projects around the park, namely design, build and install entrance signs at the East entrance to SCCC. Install and setup of current maintenance shop. Rebuild of the bridge over creek twice! Rebuild of dock, and the list goes on.

For the 2022 season the membership has climbed to 80 plus.

2018 - There were a series of meetings with the county to discuss the construction of sidewalks along 26th Ave E. On March 1st 2018 a formal meeting with county commissioners was held.

Clarke Davis, Transportation Planning Division Manager, stated 26th Avenue East is a two–lane designated thoroughfare with deep ditches on both sides. Sidewalks exist in sections on 26th Avenue East, but it is a relatively high volume road in need of continuous sidewalks. Sidewalks for 26th Avenue East have been included in half–cent infrastructure sales tax project list. The applicant will be constructing sidewalks to the logical terminus and the County will pick up the balance. The County's plan to construct sidewalks on 26th Avenue East between 27th Street

East and 45th Street East is not included in the current CIP project list.

Commissioner Benac sought confirmation that sidewalks will be constructed along the frontage of the project on 26th Avenue East with the exception of the area where the project is adjacent to wetlands. Mr. Davis displayed an aerial map to point out the County's plan to build sidewalks on 26th Avenue East and the applicant's plan to build sidewalks along the frontage of the project.

Ken Wilson, Sugar Creek Resort resident, expressed concern with the project's impact on traffic on 26th Avenue East (written comments were submitted). He also submitted comments from Peter Vellenga who was unable to attend the hearing,

Sam Hurd, Sugar Creek Resort resident, expressed concern with safety hazards on 26th Avenue East. John Zalis, Sugar Creek Country Club resident, echoed comments from Mr. Hurd. Robert Raumaugher, Sugar Creek Country Club resident, expressed similar concerns as previous speakers.

Hayden Stone, Sugar Creek Villas resident, questioned if 120 feet of right-of-way would be needed for access. Andrew Fink, area resident, reported in the past he did pursue the sidewalks for 26th Avenue East and 27th Street East. He suggested a continuous sidewalk be built along 26th Avenue East to Mixon Fruit Farms. Ken Green, Elwood Park resident, stated the project should be denied due to flooding,

Jacqueline Rowe, Sugar Creek Resort resident, expressed concern with the unsafe conditions surrounding Sugar Creek Resort. James Cochrane, Sugar Creek Estates resident, requested sidewalks on the north side of 26th Avenue East.

2022 - The sidewalks were finally built along 26th Ave. Pool repairs were completed in 2012 and 2022. The dock was repaired and the flag pole replaced with a mast from a sailing boat once owned by Norm Chastain whose lot is next to the dock. The home subdivision east of SCCC is well under way with homes being sold so the pasture long enjoyed is no more. Hurricane Ian damaged a number of units. Dick Anderson former president of the Villas died October 3.

Recollections of SCCC Owners

As the Country Club project was the last of the communities to be developed, there was interest from those who had bought into the Resort and the Estates or who camped in the old campground. The parents of **Mark Adams** were one of these couples.

"Delmer and Joan Adam camped in the Resort when it was called Sugar Creek Campgrounds. They came in the early 70's and my wife and I drove in here in Jan 1975 to visit. We came every year after that and stayed about 2 weeks every year. The park manager wore a holster and carried a good sized pistol most of the time. He claimed it was for the snakes in the creek.

We watched as the Estates were developed and my parents bought a lot in there late 1970s.

We watched the Country Club being built in early 1980s and parents bought a lot in 1983-84.

Park model companies would park their different models in the Villas- tennis court areas and have big open houses on the weekends to sell their park model homes.

In 1984 my dad and I stood on the lot that they bought on Carrotwood and could look north all the way to the pond. My exact words to him were" there's no way in hell they will sell all these lots". Boy was I wrong."

Picture of small pool in late 80s. Only pool we had for a while. My oldest daughter and son in the picture.

The Club house was the center of many various activities and one of the these was the popular Electric Corn Band. Of course in order to have any events, a good sound system was needed. These are the recollections **of Dick Anderson. (1937 -2022)**

" *When Donna and I first became part of the Sugar Creek family in 1995, I was interested in the sound system used in the clubhouse for programs, etc., so I met a gentleman named Bud McIntire (sp) who helped keep it working. At that time, the sound system consisted of an amplifier located in a cabinet near the office window. It was connected to several speaker located in the ceiling of the big room. You could plug mikes and various players into it so it was a general PA system.*

That sound system was apparently very temperamental and Bud had to fix it frequently. As the Activities Committee was trying to provide better sound facilities that could be used for a variety of functions and as some others and I were interested in playing guitar and singing for the community, I was given permission to purchase a portable sound system that would better meet our needs. It consisted of two large speakers mounted of raised pedestals and an amplifier with several inputs. We used that system for quite some time.

After a few years, some of us decided that we would also like to hold "Sock Hops" and that meant the capability of playing CDs. Activities Committee allowed me to purchase a separate system that would meet those needs. We again used that system for some time but it became apparent that a more permanent system that didn't have to be set up before and taken down after events was needed.

I found a professional sound man who serviced church's and school's sound systems and he gave us a price to install a more permanent system. It consisted of a large amplifier with many inputs and sound modification features like reverb connected to permanently mounted speakers located around the hall. I built a roll-around cabinet with drawers for microphones, cables, and other equipment to house the amp. Wireless mikes were purchased and that system is still in use today.

Over the years, several Variety (Talent) Shows have been staged by residents of the Sugar Creek Country Club and Villas. Some of us formed a "Band" we called the Electric Corn Band that played once or twice a month on Thursday evenings to provide entertainment for residents as well and folks from the Resort and Estates who wished to come. The Activities Committee set up ice cream during intermission in our performances which made for a nice evening. The number of members in the "Electric Corn Band" varies from 4 or 5 in the beginning to as many as a dozen players and singers. Some names you might recognize who were EC Band participants included Tom Green, Thelma Nicholas, Larry Squier, Dick Anderson, Russ Hubley, Tom Fingland, Bill Campbell, Earl Payne, Darcy Pitcher, Robert Browning, Myron Carter, Bob Roy, Roger Pitre, Steve Clayton. There were others like Danny Finch, Bob Hutchins, Ron Gardner, and my brother Ted Anderson, who "sat in" with the band on occasions. I'm sure I have forgotten someone but I have a leaky memory."

~~~~ The Electric Corn Band ~~~~

PHOTOS

The original Sunshine skyway before 1980

Square dancing in Sugar Creek Campground Hall 1976

Bluegrass Festival 1976

Behind bath house two at SCR, 2004

~~~~ *Bridge under water 1998* ~~~~~
~~~~ *inside SCR hall about 2000* ~~~~

~~~~ *Basket craft in CC hall and pool exercises* ~~~~

Previous page

    McLures pasture before housing went in and north end of SCCC

This page

    ~~ Spring 2022 looking west on 26th Ave E from 33rd St E entrance ~~

EPILOGUE

For those who have lived through the years of these parks there are memories to recall, names and faces and events you were a part of and for those who have arrived more recently this book tells you about the days before you drove down 26th Ave E. for the first time.

The Sugar Creek concept ownership scheme is somewhat unusual. Of the hundreds of parks in Manatee a minority (20% +/-) are owner owned and nearly all are share owned with a price tag put on the share. None of the SC shares have a value assigned. A new owner pays for a unit and lot but not for the ownership share. At the end of the day if/when whatever, a park is sold the last owner gets a cut of the sale proceeds for which they never paid a cent. So all the common area is held by the share owners, one share per lot gratuitously. So when one buys a lease this comes with it. Typically in most parks there is a share price buy in, in the tens of thousands.

Bobby Whatley and his partners set it up this way.

Could you imagine creating a club house, pool, mini golf, tennis/pickleball, shuffle today. Even then this was a hugely ambitious project evolving from what was field and bush.

You can add your own details about the story of your lot on the next page and make this book more personal to you.

No book is ever finished and I can update it as I learn more.

For now these are the stories of the Sugar Creek Communities!

Thanks for reading!

John Eacott

The story of my lot

LOT # _____ __   **PARK : SCE** __   **SCR** __ **SCCC** __

OWNERS : _____

_____

Officers of the Sugar Creek Communities
Sugar Creek Estates

1977
The first activity of the new owners was to create a social committee
Coral Methnor - President
Edith Robinson - Vice-President
Helen Willis - Secretary
"Frankie" Wolf

1978
BOARD of DIRECTORS: SOCIAL COMMITTEE:
Jeff Robinson   Pres.   Don Jung - Pres.
Walt Conover   Tres.   Joyce Lightner VP
Agnes Driggers Scty.   Inez Davidson Scty/Tres.
Warren Pearson
Bobby Whatley representing the developers

1979
Board of Directors   Recreation and Social
Jeff Robinson   Pres   Don Jung   Pres.
Walt Conover   Tres.   Joyce Lightner VP
Vern Lightner   VP   Inez Davidson   Scty/Tres.
Jim Hughes   Scty.   Harold Foster
Bobby Whatley

1980
Board of Directors   Recreation and Social
L. B. McConnell - Pres.   Eileen Rapp   Pres.
Guy Shumaker - Scty.   Betty Macauley VP
Wilford Bolce -Tres.   Helen Atkinson Scty.
Harold Foster   Charles Rapp   Tres.
Geoffrey Robinson, Roland Paquette
Bobby Whatley for the developers

1981
Board of Directors   Recreation and Social
Roland Paquette Pres.   Eileen Rapp   Pres.
Phil Fuller   VP   Betty Macauley VP

Wilford Bolce   Tres.
Guy Shumaker   Scty.
Stu Zieman, Harold Foster, Arlene King

Helen Atkinson   Scty.
Charles Rapp   Tres.

1982
Board of Directors
"Del" Adams   Pres
Bud O'Brien   VP
Guy Shumaker   Scty.
Wilford Boice   Tres.
Don Conway, Don Tower, Frank France

Recreation and Social
Ed Delke   Pres
Fay Copple   VP
Helen Atkinson   Scty.
Marvin Becksvoort   Tres.

1983
Board of Directors
Bud O'Brien   Pres
"Del" Adams   VP
Tippy Tharp   Tres.
Don Tower   Scty.
Don Conway, Frank France, Tomee Hughes
Gene Pax - replaced Del Adams who resigned

Recreation & Social
Fay Copple   Pres
Yvette Monroe   VP
Mim Turner   Scty.
Paul Smith   Tres.

1984
Board of Directors
Bud O'Brien   Pres.
Tomee Hughes   VP
Tippy Tharp   Tres.
Don Tower   Scty.
Frank France, Frank Trombley, Hank Mintz

Recreation & Social
Ed George   Pres.
Jane Donahue   VP
Mim Turner   Scty.
Paul Smith   Tres.

1985
Board of Directors
Tomee Hughes   Pres.
Pete King   VP
Tippy Tharp   Tres.
Don Tower   Scty.
Hank Mintz, Art Turner, Frank Trombley

Recreation & Social
Ed George   Pres.
Jane Donahue   VP
Mim Turner   Scty.
Paul Smith   Tres.

1986
Board of Directors
Pete King   Pres.
Hank Mintz   VP

Recreation & Social
Ed George   Pres.
Jane Donahue   VP

Tippy Tharp   Tres.
Don Tower   Scty.
Art Turner, Frank Trombley, "Red" Foote

Mim Turner   Scty.
Paul Smith   Tres.

1987
Board of Directors
Pete King   Pres.
Hank Mintz   VP
Don Tower   Scty.
Tippy Tharp   Tres.
Art Turner, Frank Trombley, "Red" Foote

Recreation & Social
Ed George   Pres.
Jane Donahue   VP
Mim Turner   Scty.
Paul Smith   Tres.

1988
Board of Directors
Hank Mintz   Pres.
"Red" Foote   VP
Charles Copple   Tres.
Don Tower   Scty.
Mary Hunter, Carl Matchett, Frank Musgrove

Recreation & Social
Ed George   Pres.
Jane Donahue   VP
Mim Turner   Scty.
Paul Smith   Tres.

1989
Board of Directors
Hank Mintz   Pres.
FrankMusgrove   VP
Charles Copple   Tres.
Don Tower   Scty.
Mary Hunter, Garl Matchett, Ralph Merrill

Recreation and Social
Della Watts   Pres.
Esther Voshell   VP
Mim Turner   Scty.
Paul Smith   Tres.

1990 - 1991
Board of Directors
Hank Mintz   Pres.
FrankMusgrove   VP
Charles Copple   Tres.
Mary Hunter   Scty.
Thomas Patterson, Garl Matchett, Ralph Merrill

Recreation and Social
DorisKing   Pres.
Tomee Hughes   VP
Alice Wood   Scty.
Paul Smith   Tres.

1991 - 1992
Board of Directors
FrankMusgrove   Pres.
Ralph Merrill   VP
Mary Hunter   Tres.

Recreation and Social
Tomee Hughes   Chair
Frances Musgrove   VC
Betty MacAuley   Scty.

Wes Symonds   Scty.   Paul Smith   Tres.
Thomas Patterson, Hank Mintz, Howard Andrews

1992 - 1993
Board of Directors		Recreation and Social	
FrankMusgrove	Pres.	Frances Musgrove	Chair
Wes Symonds	VP	Bea Andrews	VC
Mary Hunter	Tres.	Betty MacAuley	Scty.
Howard Andrews	Scty.	Paul Smith	Tres.

Thomas Patterson, Edward Coove, Warren Laird

1993 - 1994
Board of Directors		Recreation and Social	
Wes Symonds	Pres.	Bea Andrews	Chair
Warren Laird	VP	Vern Riemenschneider	VC
Mary Hunter	Tres.	Betty MacAuley	Scty.
Howard Andrews	Scty.	Paul Smith	Tres.

Ray Hisey, Edward Coover, John Tenerowicz

1994-1995
Board of Directors		Recreation and Social	
Warren Laird	Pres.	Mae Britton	Chair
Max Matchett	VP	June Overman	VC
Mary Hunter	Tres.	Mim Turner	Scty.
Nancy Drescher	Scty.	Paul Smith	Tres.

Ray Hisey, Edward Coover, John Tenerowicz

1995 - 1996
]Board of Directors		Recreation and Social	
Warren Laird	Pres.	June Overman	Chair
JohnTenerowicz	VP	Carl Brooks	VC
Mary Hunter	Tres.	Mim Turner	Scty.
Nancy Drescher	Scty.	Inez Davidson	Tres.

Ray Hisey, Ernest Kelder

1996-1997
Board of Directors		Recreation and Social	
Frank Musgrove	Pres.	Carl Brooks	Chair
Wes Symonds	VP	Edith Jones	VC
Mary Hunter	Tres.	Beryl Townsend	Scty.
Nancy Drescher	Scty.	Margaret Smith	Tres.

Paul Beyer, Miriam Turner, Jake Lavengood

NOTE: The directory for 1997-8 lists Frank Musgrove Pres., Robert Jones VP, Miriam Turner Scty, Mary Hunter Tres., Directors Vince Palange and Jake lavengood. There was an Executive Committee of Garl Matchett, John Tenerowicz, and Wes Symonds.

1997-1998

Board of Directors	Recreation and Social
Robert Jones Pres.	Delores Laird Chair
Paul Beyer VP	Darlene Carmen VC
Jake Lavengood Tres.	Beryl Townsend Scty.
Miriam Turner Scty.	Margaret Smith Tres.

Vince Palange, Byron Carmen

1998 - 1999

Board of Directors	Recreation and Social
Robert Jones Pres.	Darlene Carmen Chair
Paul Beyer VP	Henry Bailly VC
Mary Hunter Tres.	Eleanor Boback Scty.
Beryl Townsend Scty.	Margaret Smith Tres.

Vince Palange, Byron Carmen

1999 - 2000

Board of Directors	Recreation and Social
Paul Beyer Pres.	June Overman Chair
Byron Carmen VP	Henry Bailly VC
Mary Hunter Tres.	Eleanor Boback Scty.
Beryl Townsend Scty.	Margaret Smith Tres.

Vince Palange, Ray Doyle, William Martin

2000 - 2001

Board of Directors	Recreation and Social
William Martin Pres.	Erma Bowyer Chair
Ray Doyle VP	Eleanor Boback VC
Byron Carmen Tres.	Eadie Jones Scty.
Beryl Townsend Scty.	Margaret Smith Tres.

Vince Palange, Robert Jones, Roger Romesburg

2002 - **2003**
Board of Directors
William Martin Pres.
Ray Doyle VP
Byron Carmen Tres.
Beryl Townsend Scty.
Paul Beyer, John Raible, Roger Romesburg

Recreation and Social
Eleanor Boback Chair
John Raible VC
Jean Brooks Scty.
Margaret Smith Tres.

2003 - 2004
Board of Directors
Roger Romesburg Pres.
Roy Doyle VP
Beryl Townsend Scty.
Byron Carman Tres.
Paul Beyer, John Raible, Bruce Theroux, Gerald Cahalan

Recreation and Social
Erma Bowyer Chair
Bonnie Bergstresser VC
Jean Brooks Scty.
Pat Robinson Tres.

2004 -2005
Board of Directors
Roger Romesburg Pres.
Roy Doyle VP
Beryl Townsend Scty.
Byron Carman Tres.
Paul Beyer, Erma Bowyer, Bruce Theroux, Gerald Cahalan

Recreation and Social
Bonnie Bergstresser Chair
Connie Lightner VC
Jean Brooks Scty.
Pat Robinson Tres.

2005 - 2006
Board of Directors
Gerald Cahalan Pres.
Roy Doyle VP
Connie Lightner Scty.
Byron Carman Tres.

Recreation and Social
Connie Lightner Chair
Ruby Kendrick VC
Jean Brooks Scty.
Pat Robinson Tres.

2006 - 2007
Board of Directors
Gerald Cahalan Pres
Terry Lightner VP
Connie Lightner Scty.
Byron Carman Tres.
Jim Bergstresser, Erma Bowyer, Dexter Martin, Roger Romesburg

Recreation and Social
Ruby Kendrick Chair
Jean Piombino VC
Jean Brooks Scty.
Pat Robinson Tres.

2007 -2008
Board of Directors   **Recreation and Social**
Terry Lightner   Pres.   Jean Piombino   Chair
Bob Tenerowickz VP   Mary Cahalan   VC
Connie Lightner Scty. Jean Brooks   Scty.
Byron Carman   Tres. Bonnie Bergstresser   Tres.
Jim Bergstresser, Erma Bowyer, Gerald Cahalan, Dexter Martin

2008 -2009
Board of Directors   **Recreation and Social**
Terry Lightner   Pres.   Mary Cahalan   Chair
Dexter Martin   VP   Bonnie Bergstresser VC
Connie Lightner Scty. Jean Brooks   Scty.
Byron Carman   Tres. Barb Krichbaum   Tres.
Gerald Cahalan, Jim Bergstesser
Roger Romesberg, Erma Bowyer, Bob Tenerowicz

2009 -2010
Board of Directors   **Recreation and Social**
Roger Romesberg Pres.   Bonnie Bergstresser Chair
Terry Lightner   VP   Byron Carman   VC
Connie Lightner Scty. Jean Brooks   Scty.
Byron Carman   Tres. Barb Krichbaum   Tres.
Jim Bergstresser, Erma Bowyer, Carl Brooks, Gerald Cahalan

2010 - 2011
Board of Directors   **Recreation and Social**
Paul Herrewynen Pres.   Byron Carman   Chair
Gerald Cahalan   VP   Gene Shivener   VC
Harold Kendrick Scty   Scty
Carl Brooks   Tres. Bonnie Bergstresser Tres.
Jim Bergstresser, Bud Tucker

2011 - 2012
Board of Directors   **Recreation and Social**
Paul Herrewynen Pres.   Bonnie Bergstresser Chair
Gerald Cahalan   VP   Gene Shivener   VC
Harold Kendrick Scty   Sabdy Monroe   Scty
Carl Brooks   Tres. Byron Carman   Tres.
Jim Bergstresser, Bud Tucker, Erma Bowyer

2012 - 2013
Board of Directors
Jim Llewellyn   Pres.
Paul Herrewynen   VP
Erma Bowyer   Scty
Bud Tucker   Tres.
Jim Bergstresser, Carl Brooks, Gerald Cahalan

Recreation and Social
Mary Cahalan   Chair
Dee Brown   VC
Sandy Monroe   Scty
Bonnie Bergstresser   Tres.

2013 - 2014
Board of Directors
Paul Herrewynen   Pres.
John Stetzel   VP
Erma Bowyer   Scty
Terry Lightner   Tres.
Carl Brooks, Jim Bergstresser, Pat Kelly

Recreation and Social
Peggy Stetzel   Chair
Dee Brown   VC
Sandy Monroe   Scty.
Bonnie Bergstresser   Tres.

2014 - 2015
Board of Directors
Paul Herrewynen   Pres.
John Stetzel   VP
Terry Lightner   Sct/Tres.
Carl Brooks, Pat Kelly

Recreation and Social
Peggy Stetzel   Chair
Linda Slaughter   VC
Sandy Monroe   Scty.
Bonnie Bergstresser   Tres.

2015 - 2016
Board of Directors
John Stetzel   Pres.
Paul Herrewynen   VP
Terry Lightener   Scty/Tres.
Bonnie Bergstresser, Pat Kelly

Recreation and Social
Peggy Stetzel   Chair
Linda Slaughter   VC
Sandy Monroe   Scty.
Bonnie Bergstresser   Tres.

2016 - 2017
Board of Directors
John Stetzel   Pres.
Paul Herrewynen   VP
Terry Lightener   Scty/Tres.
Bonnie Bergstresser
Pat Kelly

Recreation and Social
Peggy Stetzel   Chair
Linda Slaughter   VC
Rosemary Simmers Scty.
Bonnie Bergstresser   Tres.
Judy Monts - other

2017 - 2018
Board of Directors
Bonnie Bergstresser   Pres.
Tim Slaughter   VP
Terry Lightener   Scty/Tres.
Bill Monts
John Stetzel

Recreation and Social
Peggy Stetzel   Chair
Linda Slaughter   VC
Rosemary Simmers   Scty.
Bonnie Bergstresser   Tres.
Nancy Hott   Purchasing

2018 - 2019
Board of Directors
Bonnie Bergstresser   Pres.
Tim Slaughter   VP
Terry Lightner   Sct/Tres.
Bill Monts, John Stetzel

Recreation and Social
Peggy Stetzel   Chair
Linda Slaughter   VC
Rosemary Sim   Scty.
Bonnie Bergstresser   Tres.
Nancy Hott   Purchasing

2019 - 2020
Board of Directors
Tim Slaughter   Pres.
Bill Monts   VP
Terry Lightener   Scty/Tres
Bonnie Bergstresser
Todd McConnell

Recreation and Social
Peggy Stetzel   Chair
Peach Webb   VC
Nancy Hott   Scty.
Bonnie Bergstresser   Tres.
Linda Slaughter
Rosemary Simmers

2020 - 2021
Board of Directors
Tim Slaughter   Pres.
Bill Monts   VP
Terry Lightner   Scty/Tres.
Bonnie Bergstresser,
Todd McDonnel

Recreation and Social
Peach Webb   Chair
Karen Black   VC
Nancy Hott   Scty.
Bonnie Bergstresser   Tres.

2021 - 2022
Board of Directors
Bill Monts   Pres.
Tim Slaughter   VP
Terry Lightner   Scty/Tres
Lucy Astbury, Todd McConnell

Recreation and Social
Karen Black   Chair
Linda Slaughter   VC
Nancy Hott   Scty.
Bonnie Begstresser   Tres.
Pat Montes   Committee

Sugar Creek Resort

1981, March 2 Board of Administrators
Chair Bobby Whatley
VC   Harry Moore
Scty. Katie Bennett
Tres. Bobby Whatley
       Frank Cooper
       Ralph Holland

1982

1983

1984 - Board of Administration
Pres. William Desmarias

1985
Pres. Don Clough

1986

1987
Board of Administration   **Recreation Club**
Pres. Peter Large
VP   William Grainge
Scty. Harold Virkler
Tres. Edna Mitchell
Dir. Don Clough, Dave Arnold, Roy Wallace

1988 - 89
Board of Administration   **Recreation Club**
Pres. James Bopp   Pres. Lee McLellan
VP   Bud Rusher   VP   Ardes Roberts
Scty. Ardath Dunlap   Scty. Fern Olsen
Tres.   Tres. Olin Gardner
Dir. Robert Campbell, Harold Virkler, Roy Wallace,

1990 - 1991
Board of Administrators

Pres. Bud Rusher
VP Kay Meyers
Scty. E. Jane Bopp
Tres. John Hardesty

Recreation Club - also called Sugar CreekResortSenior Citizens Service and Recreation Committee.
Pres. Rosemary Hutchins
VP Charlotte Rusher
Scty. Fern Olsen
Tres. Olin Gardner

1991 -1992
Board of Administrators
Pres.   Pres. Nancy Castleman
VP   VP Jumbo Collard
Scty. Scty. Shirley Collard
Tres. Tres. Olin Gardner

SCRCSS and RC

1992 - 1993
Board of Administrators
Pres. Ken Sinnett
VP Joyce Jennison
Scty. Ardath Dunlap
Tres. Rosemary Hutchings
Dir. Peter Large, Bud Rusher, Merry Kanthak

SCRCSS and RC
Pres. Jumbo Collard
VP
Scty. Marg Adams
Tres. Barbara Collison

Note: **February 12, 1992** the elected board was Bud Rusher President, Peter Large Treasurer and Merry Kanthak, Don Clough, Joyce Jennison, Kay Meyers, Roy Wallace. A three year term was introduced.

1993 - 1994
Board of Directors
Pres. Ken Sinnett
VP Joyce Jennison
Scty. Joyce Jennison
Tres. Rosemary Hutchins
Dir. Bud Rusher
Ardath Dunlap, Tom Kotleski

Recreation Club
Pres. Hal Virkler
VP Jumbo Collard
Scty. Marg Adams
Tres. Janice Keil
Sunshine - Tye Latinen

1994 - 1995
Board of Directors
Pres. Dick Lawson
VP Tom Hess
Scty. Joyce Jennison
Tres. Rosemary Hutchins
Dir. Don Clough
Shirley Collard, Tom Kotleski

Recreation Club
Pres. Hal Virkler
VP Jumbo Collard
Scty. Jack Holmes
Tres. Janice Keil
Sunshine   Fern Olsen

1995 - 1996
Board of Directors
Pres. Dick Lawson
VP Tom Hess
Scty. Joyce Jennison
Tres. Rosemary Hutchins

Recreation Club
Pres. Wayne Parker
VP John Lidster
Scty. Barb Leier
Tres. Janice Keil

1996 - 1997
Board of Directors
Pres. Disk Lawson
VP Joyce Jennison
Scty. Wayne Parker
Tres. Rosemary Hutchins

Recreation Club
Pres. John Lidster
VP Bob Schmidt
Scty. Barb Leir
Tres. Janice Keil

1997 - 1998
Board of Directors
Pres. Wayne Parker
VP Joyce Jennison
Scty. Ardath Dunlap
Tres. Rosemary Hutchins
Dir. Bud Rusher, Don Clough
    Gerhardt Friesma

Recreation Club
Pres. Allen Flietstra
VP Jack Herbert
Scty. Miriam Lammers
Tres. Janice Keil
Sunshine - Helen Carter

1998 - 1999
Board of Directors
Pres. Joyce Jennison
VP Rosemary Hutchins
Scty. Ardath Dunlap
Tres. Wayne Parker
    Don Clough
    Gerhardt Freisma
    Paul Bennink

Recreation Club
Chair Barb Collison
VC Bonnie Stewart
Scty. Miriam Lammers
Tres. Janice Keil
Sunshine - Helen Carter

1999 - 2000
Board of Directors
Pres. Joyce Jennison
VP   Rosemary Hutchins
Scty. Al Flietstra
Tres. Paul Bennink
Dir. Don Clough, Bud Rusher, Chuck Young

Recreation Club
Chair Barb Collison
VC Bonnie Stewart
Scty. Miriam Lammers
Tres. Janice Keil

2000 - 2001
Board of Directors
Pres. Dick Lawson
VP   Wayne Parker
Scty. Al Flietstra
Tres. Paul Bennink
Dir. Graham Brown, Bud Rusher, Bill Sheeks

Recreation Club
Chair Barb Collison
VC   Rick Molloy
Scty. Judy Brockmiller
Tres. John Hardesty

2002 - 2003
Board of Directors
Pres. Dick Lawson
VP Bud Rusher
Scty. Wayne Parker
Tres. Paul Bennink
Dir. Graham Brown, Al Flietstra, Bill Sheeks

Recreation Club
Chair Rick Molloy
VC   Connie Vadeboncoeur
Scty. Judy Brockmiller
Tres. John Hardesty

2003 - 2004
Board of Directors
Pres. Dick Lawson
VP   Bud Rusher
Scty. Wayne Parker
Tres. Paul Bennink
Dir. Graham Brown, Al Flietstra, Bill Sheeks

Recreation Club
Chair Rick Molloy
VC   Connie Vadeboncoeur
Scty. Judy Brockmiller
Tres. John Hardesty

2004 - 2005
Board of Directors
Pres. Dick Lawson
VP   Bud Rusher
Scty. Wayne Parker
Tres. Paul Bennink
Dir. Graham Brown, Fred Evans, Bill Sheeks

Recreation Club
Chair Rick Molloy
VC   Doug Pratt
Scty. Judy Brockmiller
Tres. John Hardesty

2005 -2006
Board of Directors
Pres. Dick Lawson
VP Bud Rusher
Scty. Wayne Parker
Tres. Paul Bennink
Dir. Jim Meyer, Fred Evans, Bill Sheeks

Recreation Club
Chair Dave Patchkowski
VC   Doug Pratt
Scty. Judy Brockmiller
Tres. John Hardesty

2006 - 2007
Board of Directors
Pres. Paul Bennink
VP   Jim Meyer
Scty. Ron Fletcher
Tres. Rick Molloy
Dir. Wayne Parker, Dick Lawson, Bill Sheeks

Recreation Club
Chair Dave Patchkowski
VC   John Eacott
Scty. Judy Brockmiller
Tres. John Hardesty

2007 - 2008
Board of Directors
Pres. Paul Bennink
VP Jim Meyer
Scty. Ron Fletcher
Tres. Rick Molloy
Dir. Burt Zuege, Fred Evans, Ken Wilson

Recreation Club
Chair John Eacott
VC Dave Patchkowski
Scty. Kathy Wilson
Tres. John Hardesty

2008 - 2009
Board of Directors
Pres. Rick Molloy
VP   Ken Wilson
Scty. Ron Fletcher
Tres. Becky Hayes
Dir. Burt Zuege, Fred Evans, Bud Rusher

Recreation Club
Chair John Eacott
VC   Dave Patchkowski
Scty. Kathy Wilson
Tres. John Hardesty

2009 - 2010
Board of Directors
Pres. Ken Wilson
VP   Bud Rusher
Scty/Tres. Becky Hayes
Dir. Burt (Burton) Zuege
Fred Evans, Bill Vesters, Yoland Carrier

Recreation Club
Chair John Eacott
VC   Herb Zuercher
Scty. Kathy Wilson
Tres, John Hardesty

2010 - 2011

Board of Directors	Recreation Club
Pres. Ken Wilson	Chair John Eacott
VP Jim Meyer	VC Dianna Brabson
Scty. Becky Hayes	Scty. Kathy Wilson
Tres. Rick Molloy	Tres. John Hardesty

Dir. Bill Vesters, Yoland Carrier, Dave Powers

2011 - 2012

Board of Directors	Recreation Club
Pres. Ken Wilson	Chair John Eacott
VP Bill Vesters	VC Dianna Brabson
Scty. Carol McLeod	Scty. Kathy Wilson
Tres. Rick Molloy	Tres. John Hardesty

Dir. Yoland Carrier, Dave Powers, Ron Fletcher

2012 - 2013

Board of Directors	Recreation Club
Pres. Ken Wilson	Chair John Eacott
VP Bill Vesters	VC - Iona Swartzentruber
Scty. Carol McLeod	Scty. Kathy Wilson
Tres. Rick Molloy	Tres. Herb Zuercher

Dir. Yoland Carrier, Nancy Berens, Ron Fletcher

2013 - 2014

Board of Directors	Recreation Club
Pres. Ken Wilson	Chair John Eacott
VP Bill Vesters	VC Dave Patchkowski
Scty. Carol McLeod	Scty. Kathy Wilson
Tres. Rick Molloy	Tres. Don McLeod

Dir. Yoland Carrier, Nancy Berens, Ron Fletcher

2014 - 2015

Board of Directors	Recreation Club
Pres. Ken Wilson	Chair John Eacott
VP Bill Vesters	VC Dave Patchkowski
Scty. Carol McLeod	Scty. Kathy Wilson
Tres. Herb Zuercher	Tres. Don McLeod

Dir. Nancy Berens, Ron Fletcher, Jack Morris

2015 - 2016
Board of Directors   Recreation Club
Pres. Ken Wilson   Chair John Eacott
VP   Bill Vesters   VC   Dave Patchkowski
Scty. Carol McLeod   Scty. Kathy Wilson
Tres. Herb Zuercher   Tres. Don McLeod
Dir. Nancy Berens, Ron Fletcher, Jack Morris

2016 - 2017
Board of Directors   Recreation Club
Pres. Ken Wilson   Chair John Eacott
VP   Bill Vesters   VC   Rauline Morris
Scty. Carol McLeod   Scty. Kathy Wilson
Tres. Herb Zuercher   Tres. Don McLeod
Dir. Nancy Berens
Dir/Asst.Tres - Rinus DeKlerk, Dir. Jack Morris

2017 - 2018
Board of Directors   Recreation Club
Pres. Ken Wilson   Chair Rauline Morris
VP   Jack Morris   VC   Don McLeod
Scty. Carol McLeod   Scty.. Kathy Wilson
Tres. Herb Zuercher   Tres. Ken Zuercher
Dir. Nancy Berens   MAL   Irene Butler
Dir.Asst.Tres - Rinus DeKlerk, Dir. John Butler

2018 - 2019
Board of Directors   Recreation Club
Pres. Ken Wilson   Chair Rauline Morris
VP   Jack Morris   VC   Don McLeod
Scty. Carol McLeod   Scty. Kathy Wilson
Tres. Herb Zuercher   Tres. Ken Zeurcher
Dir. Nancy Berens   MAL   Irene Butler
Dir/Asst.Tres - Rinus DeKlerk, Dir. John Butler

2019 - 2020
Board of Directors   Recreation Club
Pres. Herb Zuercher   Chair Rauline Morris
VP   Mike Percell   VC   Don McLeod
Scty. Jack Morris   Scty. Leslie Pelkofer
Tres. Ria Davids   Tres. Don Czubak

Dir.   Carol McLeod   MAL Irene Butler
Dir.   John Miller, John Butler

2020 - 2021
Board of Directors   **Recreation Club**
Pres. Herb Zuercher   Chair Rauline Morris
VP   Mike Percell   VC   Don McLeod
Scty. Jack Morris   Scty. Leslie Pelkofer
Tres. Ria Davids   Tres. Donna Percy
Dir.   Carol McLeod   MAL   Irene Butler
Dir.   John Miller, Jennifer Wilcox

2021 - 2022

Board of Directors   **Recreation Club**
Pres. Herb Zuercher   Chair Rauline Morris
VP   Jennifer Wilcox   VC   Greg Kissell
Scty. Jack Morris   Scty. Leslie Pelkofer
Tres. Tom Buckhannon   Tres. Donna Percy
Dir.   Carol McLeod, John Miller, Mark Sanders

2022 - 2023
Board of Directors   **Recreation Club**
Pres. Jennifer Wilcox   Chair Rauline Morris
VP   Jack Morris   VC   Greg Kissell
Scty. Herb Zuercher   Scty. Leslie Pelkofer
Tres. Tom Buckhannon   Tres. Donna Percy
Dir.   John Miller, Connie Vellenga
Dir.   Jeff Tackett

Sugar Creek Country Club

It is not known if the advisory council existed before 1988. There were 131 owners in 1988. Joe Schmidt was appointed in 1985 to represent the owners. In 1986 or 1987 Harold Fisher was elected by the owners.

1988

SCCC Board
Charles Bencin Pres.
Don Bencin VP
Harold Fisher elected by owners

SCCC Advisory Council
Chair Tom Dale
VC   Del Adams
Scty. Helen De Back
Tres. Marg Miller
Walter Bouchard
Merle Richee
Wallace Miller
John Crotty

1990 -1991

Executive Committee
Charles Bencin Pres.
Don Bencin
Harold Fisher

SCCC Advisory Council
Chair Del Adams
VC   Bill Roy
Scty. Betty Schlough
Tres. Walter Bouchard

Activity
Russell Helmer
Ken Moore
Merle Richee
Keith Torkelson

1991 - 1992

Board of Directors
Pres/Treas. George Howland
VP/Scty. Russell Helmer
Owner/board member Don Bencin

Operating Board
Chair Ben Pfeiffer
Activities Ruth Hart
Asst. Treas. Elmer Russell
Asst. Chairs Bill Roy and Walt McCormick

1992 - 1993
Owners Charles Bencin Pres. Don Bencin Treas.

SCCC Board **Executive Committee**
Pres. George Howland   George Howland
VP Russell Helmer   Bill Roy
Scty. Betty Schlough   Merle Richee
Tres. Elmer Russell   There were 18 sub committees
 Dir. Ben Pfeiffer, Merle Ritchee, Bill Roy

1993 - 1994
SCCC Board **Activities**
Pres. Russ Helmer   Director Elmer Russell
VP   Joan Beckley   Asst. Dir. Ruby Russell
Scty. Ken Moore   Tres.   Vera Stilson
Tres. Rosemary Aumaugher
Dir. George Howland, Bill Roy, Howard Millard

BOARD of DIRECTORS 1993 - 1994
HOWARD MILLARD - KEN MOORE - BILL ROY - (RUSSELL HELMER) - ROSEMARY AUMAUGHER - JOAN BECKLEY &
(PRESIDENT) TREASURER VICE PRESIDENT
GEORGE HOWLAND

1994 - 1995
SCCC Board Activities
Pres. Joan Beckley Director Elmer Russell
VP   Howard Millard Asst. Dir. Ruby Russell
Scty. Carolyn Gordon Tres. Vera Stilson
Tres. Delmer Adams
Dir. Howard Brouwer, Arthur Shaw, Edward Stilson

1995 - 1996
SCCC Board Activities
Pres. Joan Beckley Director Elmer Russell
VP   Edward Stilson Asst. Dir. Ruby Russell
Scty. Carolyn Gordon Tres. Vera Stilson
Tres. Jerry Johnson
Dir. Howard Brouwer, Arthur Shaw, Augie Turner

1996 - 1997
SCCC Board Activities
Pres. Edward Stilson Director Russ Helmer
VP   George Leach Tres.   Vera Stilson
Scty. Helen O'Brien
Tres./asst. Scty. Jerry Johnson
Dir. Howard Brouwer, John Pettinger, Augie Turner

1997 - 1998
SCCC Board Activities
Pres. George Leach Director Tom Roberts
VP   Al Sweet Tres.   Vera Stilson
Scty. Helen O'Brien
Tres./asst. Scty Rosemary Aumaugher
Dir. Edward Stilson, Ray Jarvis, Bob Roy

1998 - 1999
SCCC Board Activities
Pres. George Leach Director Tom Roberts
VP   Al Sweet Tres.   Vera Stilson
Scty. Helen O'Brien
Tres. Bob Roy
Dir. Edward Stilson, Ray Jarvis, Tom Roberts

1999 - 2000
SCCC Board   **Activities**
Pres. George Leach   Director Tom Roberts
VP   Ray Jarvis   Tres.   Vera Stilson
Scty. Edward Stilson
Tres. Bob Roy
Dir.   Dick La Valley, Dan Finch, Tom Roberts

2000 -2001
SCCC Board of Directors: **Activities**
Pres. George Leach   Director Tom Roberts
VP.   Dan Finch   Tres.   Vera Stilson
Scty. Helen O'Brien
Tres. Bob Roy
Dir.   Frank Wood, Bill Beckley, Tom Roberts

Note: At about this time the SCCC expanded it's organization to include Park Services, Senior Citizen Services, and Activities programs. This system continued to evolve and included many more people which added too many participants to continue listing them here.

2001 - 2002
SCCC Board of Dir.
Pres. George Leach
VP.   Dan Finch
Scty. Helen O'Brien

Tres: Bob Roy
Ass't Tres/Ass't Scty. Frank Wood
Dir.   Bill Beckley, Tom Roberts

2002 - 2003
SCCC Board of Dir.
Pres. Dan Finch
VP   Tom Roberts
Scty. Helen O'Brien
Tres. Frank Wood
Ass't Tres/Ass't Scty. Sally Cronin
Dir.   Darcy Pitcher, Richard LaValley

2003 - 2004
SCCC Board of Dir.
Pres. Dan Finch
VP. Tom Roberts
Scty. Helen Koedoot
Tres. Sally Cronin
Dir. Bob Hutchins, Richard LaValley

2004 - 2005
SCCC Board of Dir.
Pres. Dan Finch
VP. Tom Roberts
Scty. Helen Koedoot
Tres. Sally Cronin
Dir. Bob Hutchins, Darcy Pitcher, Richard LaValley

2005 - 2006
SCCC Board of Dir.
Pres. Tom Roberts
VP. Bob Hutchins
Scty. Helen Koedoot
Tres. Sally Cronin
Dir. Bob Baker, Ron Brown, Dick Anderson

2006 - 2007
SCCC Board of Dir.
Pres. Bob Baker
VP. Dick Anderson
Scty. Helen Koedoot
Tres. Sally Cronin
Dir. Ron Brown, Carl Beatty, Jim Johnston

2007 - 2008
SCCC Board of Dir.
Pres. Bob Baker
VP. Dick Anderson
Scty. Helen Koedoot
Tres. Sally Cronin
Dir. Ron Brown, Carl Beatty, Jim Johnston

2008 - 2009
SCCC Board of Dir.
Pres. Bob Baker
VP. Dick Anderson
Scty. Helen Koedoot
Tres. Sally Cronin
Dir. Dan Finch, Dave Wingo Jerry Johnson

2009 - 2010
SCCC Board of Dir.
Pres. Bob Baker
VP. Dick Anderson
Scty. Helen Koedoot
Tres. Sally Cronin
Dir. Dan Finch, Jack George, Jerry Johnson

2010 - 2011
SCCC Board of Dir.
Pres. Bob Baker
VP. Dick Anderson
Scty. Helen Koedoot
Tres. Sally Cronin
Dir. Tom Fingland, Jack George, Jerry Johnson

2011 - 2012
SCCC Board of Dir.
Pres. Bob Baker
VP. Dick Anderson
Scty. Helen Koedoot
Tres. Sally Cronin
Dir. Tom Fingland, Carl Beatty, Earl Edwards

2012 - 2013
SCCC Board of Dir.
Pres. Bob Baker
VP. Dick Anderson
Scty. Helen Koedoot
Tres. Sally Cronin
Dir. Tom Fingland, Earl Edwards, Phyllis Szulczewski

2013 - 2014
SCCC Board of Dir.
Pres. Bill Watts
VP.   Dick Anderson
VP.   John Zalis
Scty. Helen Koedoot
Tres. Phyllis Szulczewski
Dir.   Earl Edwards, Tom Fingland

2014 -2015
SCCC Board of Dir.
Pres. Bill Watts
VP.   John Zalis
Scty. Barbara Fish
Ass't Scty   Helen Koedoot
Tres. Phyllis Szulczewski
Ass't Tres. Linda Shippee
director.   Hayden Stone

2015 - 2016
SCCC Board of Dir.
Pres. Bill Watts
VP.   John Zalis
Scty. Barbara Fish
Ass't Scty. Hayden Stone
Tres. Phyllis Szulczewski
Ass't Tres: Linda Shippee
Dir.   Pauline Halbert

2016 - 2017
SCCC Board of Dir.
Pres. John Zalis
VP.   Hayden Stone
Scty. Barbara Fish
Tres. Phyllis Szulczewski
Ass't Tres. Linda Shippee
Dir.   Pauline Halbert, Bob Maclarty

2017 - 2018
SCCC Board of Dir.
Pres. Pauline Halbert

VP. John Zalis
Scty. Barbara Fish
ass't Scty   Hayden Stone
Tres. Phyllis Szulczewski
ass't Tres. Linda Shippee   Dir. Dan DeMaio

2018 - 2019
SCCC Board of Dir.
Pres. Pauline Halbert
VP. John Zalis
Scty. Barbara Fish
Ass't Scty. Hayden Stone
Tres. Phyllis Szulczewski
ass't Tres. Linda Shippee   Dir. Dan DeMaio

2019 - 2020
SCCC Board of Dir.
Pres. Pauline Halbert
VP. John Zalis
Scty. Barbara Fish
ass't Scty. Hayden Stone
Tres. Phyllis Szulczewski
Ass't Tres. Linda Shippee   Dir. Dan DeMaio

2020 -2021
SCCC Board of Dir.
Pres. Pauline Halbert
VP. Joe Lewien
Scty. Barbara Fish
Ass't Scty. Dan DeMaio
Tres. Phyllis Szulczewski
Ass't Tres. Linda Shippee   Dir. John Geertsema

2021 - 2022
SCCC Board of Dir.
Pres. John Geertsema
VP. Joe Lewien
Scty. Barbara Fish   Ass't Scty. Cherie Watson
Tres. Joe Lewien   Ass't Tres. Linda Shippee,
Dir: John Vanderploeg
Dir: Dan DeMaio,

Sugar Creek Villas

The Sugar Creek Villas used the services of a management company. However from at least 1992 they had elected officials and an annual meeting.

1992- 1993, 1993 - 1994, 1994 - 1995,

Pres. Jerry Fink
VP. Ken Wertz
Scty. Lou Whitmer

1995 - 1996

Kenneth Lohstroh
Phil Parisian
Patricia Bencin

1996 - 1997,
Pres. Phil Parisian
V.P, Lou Whitmer
Scty/T. Dick Anderson

1997 and 1998 -1999
Phil Parisian
Barbara Bosse
Dick Anderson

1999 - 2000, 2000 - 2001,
Pres. Thomas Moore
V.P, Jerry Briggs
Scty/T. Dick Anderson

2001 - 2002
Dick Anderson
Dean McDonald
Charles Sandway

2002-2003
Pres. Dick Anderson
VP. Dean McDonald
Scty/T. Bill Campbell

www.ingramcontent.com/pod-product-compliance
Lightning Source LLC
Chambersburg PA
CBHW040312170426
43195CB00020B/2939